THE LOVE NEST

A FARCICAL COMEDY IN TWO ACTS

by

RAYMOND HOPKINS

HANBURY PLAYS

**Keeper's Lodge, Broughton Green
Droitwich, Worcestershire WR9 7EE**

BY THE SAME AUTHOR

LOVE BEGINS AT FIFTY
IT MUST BE LOVE

THE LOVE NEST

© Raymond Hopkins 2002

ISBN:- 185205 258 9

PEERFORMING RIGHTS

The author of THE LOVE NEST, Raymond Hopkins, is donating his share of the proceeds to MULTIPLE SCLEROSIS RESEARCH.

THE LOVE NEST

The Longthorps live in a small town on the South Coast of England. It is late spring – the present day. The play takes place in the kitchen and adjacent dining room of a guest house.

THE SETTINGS

THE KITCHEN

This occupies a quarter of the stage on the actors' right. As is the furniture in the dining area, the units are years out of date. (This should provide very little problem as the companies who fit new kitchens are often delighted to get rid of the old units they take out.) To avoid masking, the dividing wall should be cut away slightly above the height of the two low level units on actors' left of the kitchen area. There is a space between them which passes for the door leading into the dining area. There are two units on the opposite wall, one of which is the cupboard used for the message. On the back wall is a sink unit with practical cold water, a cooker (non-practical) and a fridge (non-practical except for a light which comes on when it is opened). All the cupboards should have various items in them as they are opened by the health inspector several times. Other practical items include a toaster, coffee and tea making equipment – all on the upstage surfaces. Dressing should include enough pans, plates, cups etc. to give a cluttered effect. There is a door upstage, on the far right wall.

THE DINING ROOM

There are four separate tables with three chairs round each. The one against the actors' left wall remains empty throughout the action. They are covered with rather drab tablecloths. There is a small hi-fi unit on a table down left. An old sideboard backs onto the upstage kitchen unit. This serves as a limited bar and a resting place for magazines and seaside brochures. There is a table on the upstage wall which acts as a reception desk. Behind it is a board with pigeon-holes and hooks for room keys. On the desk is a phone, an appointment book, a visitors' book and a service bell etc. There are prints on the walls and such dressing as is thought appropriate. The general effect is of rooms which have hardly altered in several decades. There is an exit to the hall on the back wall, left of the desk. The pace of the play can be accelerated by having two separate hall exits. One with stairs, for internal access and the other for external access.

CAST IN ORDER OF APPEARANCE

JACK LONGTHORP   (Guest house proprietor) About fifty-three. A big thinker, and an opportunist. Smart in appearance. He has many mood swings. Does not always think before he speaks.

MARY LONGTHORP   About forty-nine. Has been married to Jack for twenty years. Slightly overweight. Does not make the best of herself. She is a quiet person, who lacks self-confidence. Her life is centred around the guest house.

TINA LEWIS   About thirty-three. Slim and very attractive. She has had lots of boy friends, but never got serious with any of them. A bit scatty. Could be described as a dumb blonde. Very likeable. She has a zest for living life to the full.

JANET THOMPSON   About fifty-three. Has been dominated by her mother all her life. She is smartly dressed and well spoken. At times she acts like a snob. She has an affectionate side to her character which has been suppressed.

MARJORIE BRAITHWAITE   (Mother of Janet) About seventy-eight. She is a cantankerous harridan, who thinks the world revolves around her. She gives the appearance of being wealthy, but she is not. She is a hypochondriac. In her opinion, her daughter has married beneath herself.

DAVID THOMPSON   About fifty-five. An intelligent, thoughtful person, who is a romantic at heart. He is well groomed, and looks good for his age. Normally placid, but is becoming increasingly frustrated with his mother-in-law.

SARA ROSS   About twenty-two. She is petite, and good looking. A likeable, outgoing girl with lots of friends, and interests. She has a high sex drive. Just married Duncan.

DUNCAN ROSS   About twenty-five. Very well built, and good looking. He likes all sports, but his main love is rugby. He is super fit. However, we do not see him at his best. He is scared of mice.

AMINA BETNAY   About forty-two. Slim, attractive and intelligent. Has been looking for love but without success. Money is no object, and it shows. She is one of life's high-flyers.

TONI CLARK   About thirty-nine. Well spoken and smartly dressed. She is slightly overweight. Comes across as brash, but has a very caring side to her nature.

TYSON   The mouse.

5

ACT I

Scene I

As the curtain rises, Mary is in the kitchen making herself busy. Jack enters from hall. He looks through appointment book, shakes his head, then goes into kitchen.

JACK   Do you realise we're half-empty this week?

MARY   You mean half-full, darling. Try and be positive.

JACK   How can I? We haven't got a single reservation for October. *(Pause)* When we got married and first took on this guest house, they were queuing at the door with their buckets and spades. I rang the Samaritans last week, I'd got so desperate.

MARY   Did any of them want to book a holiday?

JACK   I wasn't looking for customers. I wanted someone to help me through this crisis.

(Tina enters from hall and goes into kitchen. She is wearing a raincoat)

MARY   Things can only get better.

TINA   Afternoon, all. It's raining cats and dogs out there.

JACK   Great, they say it never rains but it pours.

TINA   *(Taking off her raincoat and hanging it up)* What have I said?

MARY   Take no notice of him, Tina. He's wallowing in self-pity.

TINA   Well I've got some news that'll cheer you up. The local travel agents are offering ten days in Spain for only two hundred quid.

JACK   Has anybody got a gun?

MARY   If things are that bad, do something about it.

JACK   Like what? Phone the Almighty and ask if He'll point the sun in our direction?

MARY   All right, we can't do anything about the weather, but at least we can give our guests a memorable holiday.

JACK   So what are you suggesting – I get some scaffolding, so Tina can pole dance whilst serving the Sunday roast?

TINA   *(Indignantly)* Here, what sort of girl do you think I am?

MARY   Just ignore him, Tina.

TINA   In any case, you'd need to get proper poles. That scaffolding'd be far too rough. *(Rubbing her inner thighs)*

JACK   We might as well face facts, the English guest house went out with the sixties. *(Pause)* In those days, they were full to capacity.

TINA   Let's turn the clocks back. *(Pause)* If the swinging sixties were the heyday of the guest house, we'll recreate them.

JACK   What are you babbling on about?

TINA   Let's have a day reliving the sixties. My dad was always saying how great they were.

MARY   Actually, that's not such a bad idea.

TINA   We'll get all the guests involved. It'd be a laugh.

MARY   We could all dress up in sixties gear.

TINA   We could play the sixties hits.

MARY   We'll serve expresso coffee.

JACK   *(Getting enthusiastic)* This might just work.

MARY   I've got several posters of pop groups from that era. That'd add some authenticity.

TINA   We could charge sixties prices for everything. That'd add authenticity.

JACK   Don't let's get too carried away.

MARY   It'd be fantastic, going back to those fun-filled days.

JACK   Yes, it would. *(Pause)* I'm glad I thought of it.

(Janet enters from hall. She is helping her mother, Marjorie, who has a walking stick and seems to be having difficulty in getting about. Tina, Jack and Mary continue to go about their duties in the kitchen in silent conversation)

JANET   Take it easy, Mother, there's no rush.

MARJORIE   I can't see why we didn't stay in a proper hotel.

JANET   You know the reason. David and I had our honeymoon here thirty-two years ago. He thought it'd be nice to come back. *(Pause)* He's such a romantic.

MARJORIE   Don't you mean cheapskate? *(Pause)* How could he bring you to such a grotesque place?

JANET   We had a lovely week.

MARJORIE   I've always said you married beneath yourself.

DAVID   *(Entering from hall, carrying three large suitcases)* It's not changed a bit. *(Puts cases on floor and looks around room)*

MARJORIE   No, I'd say that wallpaper's been here since the place was built.

7

JANET   It's all coming back to me now. *(Looking thoughtful)* Every evening we'd walk along the front with a bag of chips.

MARJORIE   *(To David)* I suppose that saved you buying a meal.

DAVID   *(Getting close to Janet)* You were the prettiest girl on the promenade.

JANET   Thank you, darling. You weren't so bad looking yourself.

DAVID   Didn't we have a fantastic time?

JANET   We were experiencing uncontrollable happiness. *(Janet and David look into each others eyes)*

MARJORIE   I'm experiencing uncontrollable flatulence after being cramped in that car. *(Whoopee cushion?)* I need a loo.

(Marjorie rings the service bell. Jack goes into dining room from kitchen)

DAVID   Hello, we're booked in for the week.

JACK   I trust you had a good journey?

MARJORIE   No we didn't, the traffic on the motorway was horrendous. *(Glaring at David)* Mind you, we always sit in the stationary lane while the others are moving freely.

DAVID   *(Ignoring Marjorie)* We stopped here thirty-two years ago on honeymoon.

JANET   So we decided to come back and relive those happy days.

JACK   What a wonderful idea.

MARJORIE   *(Aside)* What a load of drivel.

DAVID   By the way, this is Janet and I'm David Thompson.

JANET   *(Shaking hands)* Pleased to meet you.

DAVID   We've also brought Marjorie, my mother-in-law. *(Looking extremely fed up)* She's been living with us for the past ten years.

JACK   Jack Longthorp, the proprietor. *(Goes to shake hands with Marjorie, but she does not respond)*

MARJORIE   You can call me Mrs Braithwaite.

JACK   *(Looking through appointment book and taking two keys from the board)* Right, you're in rooms five and six. I'll show you where they are and then we'll have a welcoming cup of tea ready. *(Pause)* If you'd follow me.

(Jack exits to hall. Janet and Marjorie follow. David picks up the three cases and struggles through hall exit)

MARY   I've never seen Jack so depressed.

TINA   He's probably going through the mid-life crisis.

MARY   More like the mid-season crisis, due to lack of bookings.

TINA   We'll soon get things moving.

MARY   I do hope so. We've sacrificed everything for this guest house. *(Pause)* It'd be a shame to see it go under now.

(Sara and Duncan enter from hall. Duncan looks dishevelled. Sara is carrying their suitcase in one hand and supporting Duncan with the other. Sara rings the bell)

TINA   I'll go. *(Goes into dining room)*. Hello, may I help?
SARA   Hi, Sara and Duncan Ross; we're booked in for the week.
TINA   *(Looking through appointment book and taking key from the board)* You're in room one. *(In an excited voice)* Oh, that's the honeymoon suite.
SARA   *(Duncan rests his head on Sara's shoulder)* Duncan's a bit worn out, at the moment.
TINA   Has the journey been awful?
SARA   No, his stupid rugby mates kept forcing drinks down him at the reception. He wasn't fit for anything last night.
TINA   Oh dear. *(Pause)* Let's hope he'll sleep well tonight.
SARA   *(Getting cross)* He'd better not.
TINA   I'll show you to your room. Then we're all meeting for a cup of tea. *(Pause)* If you'd follow me.

(Tina exits to hall followed by Sara and Duncan. Jack enters from hall and goes into kitchen)

JACK   *(Imitation of Humphrey Bogart)* Why, in all the guest houses, in all the towns, does she have to walk into mine?
MARY   Who are you on about?
JACK   Marjorie Braithwaite, the wrinkly whose sole aim this week'll be to make my life unbearable.

(Tina enters from hall and goes into kitchen. Jack starts making the tea)

TINA   That Duncan Ross'll never keep up with his wife's insatiable appetite.
MARY   They're on honeymoon, aren't they?
TINA   Yes, and she's going to kill him before the week's out.
JACK   You're talking rubbish. The male species is more than capable of gratifying all female demands.
MARY   That's a laugh, coming from you.
TINA   I'll bet you within a couple of days he'll be on his knees begging for mercy.
JACK   Get real, Tina. When it comes to making love, men are like rabbits.

9

MARY   (Sarcastically) Only in your case it was all rabbit and no action.
JACK   I can assure you that the male libido's the most potent force in the universe.
TINA   So why don't you put your money where your mouth is?
JACK   All right, let's make it twenty quid. The only thing is we'll need to monitor his energy levels.
TINA   Actually, they've just told me he's a rugby player. I'm not so sure about this.
JACK   I knew you'd chicken out.
TINA   But these rugby players spend half their lives doing press-ups and squat thrusts.
JACK   That's it. If he's got the energy to do ten press-ups at the end of the week, it'll be pay-out time for you.
TINA   (Shaking hands with Jack) You've got yourself a bet.
MARY   Right, we can't stand here all day gossiping. Tina, would you give me a hand with the linen?
TINA   Okay.

(Tina and Mary exit to hall. After a few seconds, Marjorie enters from hall and rings service bell. Jack goes into dining room)

MARJORIE   When did you last change the sheets?
JACK   This morning, Mrs Braithwaite.
MARJORIE   In that case it's about time you changed your laundry.
JACK   I'll bear that in mind. (Pause) Was there anything else?
MARJORIE   Where's the switch for the air conditioning in my room?
JACK   (Getting cross) There's a lever on the window marked 'lift to open.' (Pause) Is that all Marjorie, I mean madam?
SARA   (Entering from hall with Duncan) We love the room, and the sea view.
JACK   Thank you. (To Duncan) I hear you're a rugby player. Do you work out much?
DUNCAN   I always start the day with fifty press-ups.
JACK   Excellent.
MARJORIE   I'm still waiting for my tea.
JACK   Right, won't be a moment. (Jack goes into kitchen) I'm going to kill that woman.

(Jack makes the tea. Sara and Duncan sit at a table)

SARA   (Trying to make conversation) We're on our honeymoon. We got married yesterday.

MARJORIE   So when's the baby due?

(Duncan looks at Sara with a horrified expression)

SARA   *(Getting cross)* I'm not having a baby.
MARJORIE   I thought that's the only reason people got married nowadays. In my day there was no hanky-panky until you'd got wed.
DUNCAN   *(Aside)* Who'd want to wed an old slapper like you?
MARJORIE   Pardon?
SARA   *(Kicking Duncan)* Duncan said, did you have a slap-up do?
MARJORIE   My husband left me ten years ago. He ran off to Tenerife with our local lollipop lady.
SARA   I am sorry.
MARJORIE   Not half as sorry as I was. The poor kids haven't got anyone to see them over the road now.
DAVID   *(Entering from hall with Janet)* Hello, we've not been introduced. This is Janet, and I'm David.
SARA   Hi, Sara and Duncan.

(They all shake hands)

DAVID   And you've obviously met my mother-in-law, Marjorie.
MARJORIE   *(Looking at Duncan)* Doesn't have much to say does he? What is he, the strong, silent type?
DUNCAN   I don't feel too good. *(Rushing through hall exit almost throwing up)*
SARA   *(Looking embarrassed)* He drank too much at the reception.
MARJORIE   They've just got married.
JANET   Best of luck.
DAVID   *(Aside – looking at Marjorie)* You're going to need it.
JACK   *(Goes into dining room, carrying tea)* Tea up.
MARJORIE   About time. I could have died of thirst.
JACK   *(Aside)* We can all live in hope. *(Handing everyone a cup of tea)*
JANET   Thank you. That's just what the doctor ordered.
MARJORIE   *(Looking at her tea)* It looks like something Doctor Crippin ordered.
JACK   Welcome to *Sea View*, and thank you for choosing us. *(Pause)* We'll do our very best to provide for your every need. If you've any questions, don't hesitate to ask.
MARJORIE   Who do we see about getting a refund?
JANET   Mother, please.
SARA   Have you got any entertainment?

11

JACK   *(Looking pleased with himself)* We certainly have. On Friday, with no expense spared, we'll be reliving 'The Swinging Sixties.'

SARA   What's 'The Swinging Sixties?'

JACK   It was a time of free love, flowerpower, and new fashions. In those days a threepenny joey would get you a cup of tea, and ten bob would get you paralytic.

DAVID   There was a revolution in pop music.

MARJORIE   Everybody was on strike.

JANET   *(Looking at David)* They were wonderful times. Everything was new and exciting. We didn't seem to have a care in the world.

DAVID   *(Looking at Janet)* We lived life to the full.

JACK   I'll give you all the details later. *(Pause)* Right, I expect you'll all be wanting to get out and enjoy that bracing sea air.

MARJORIE   It's blowing a gale out there. I could be washed out to sea.

JACK   *(Sarcastically)* That would be a shame.

SARA   I'd better go and check on Duncan.

JACK   He might fancy a cup of Horlicks tonight.

SARA   No thanks, he certainly won't be suffering from night starvation. *(Exits to hall)*

JANET   Come on, Mum, let's get you settled in.

DAVID   I'll get the rest of our things out of the car.

(Janet, Marjorie and David exit to hall. Jack picks up empty tea cups and goes into kitchen. After a few seconds, Tina enters from hall and goes into kitchen)

TINA   How did the welcome meeting go?

JACK   They seemed to warm to the idea of having a sixties day.

TINA   What are the guests like? I've only met the young honeymoon couple.

JACK   The Thompsons are nice, but they've brought the mother-in-law from hell.

TINA   That's why I've stayed single. You've no relatives to worry about.

(Amina Betnay enters from hall. She is wearing a raincoat and carrying an umbrella. She rings the service bell)

JACK   If that's Marjorie Braithwaite again, I'll throttle her. *(Goes into dining room)* Oh, hello.

AMINA   Amina Betnay. I've a reservation.

JACK *(Looking through appointment book)* So it's Ms. Betnay? Plus a friend, Mr Stoker. *(Pause)* Is he parking the car?

AMINA No, he's in the South of France.

JACK What happened? Did he lose his way?

AMINA He's not the charmer I thought he was. We've split.

JACK Another guest bites the dust. *(Jack crosses name from book. He then takes a key from the board)* You're in room seven. I'll get Tina to show you to your room. *(Shouting)* Tina, would you show Ms. Betnay to room seven?

TINA *(Tina goes into dining room. Jack hands her the key)* Yes, certainly. If you'd like to follow me.

JACK I'd better come and set the heating on max.

(Tina, Amina and Jack exit to hall. After a few seconds, David enters from hall. He walks around dining room and then goes into the kitchen to a cupboard and opens the door. He looks inside cupboard)

JANET *(Off)* David, where are you? *(Enters from hall)*

DAVID *(Poking about in cupboard)* I'm in the kitchen.

JANET *(Goes into kitchen)* What are you doing?

DAVID I'm looking for something. *(Pause)* Think back to our honeymoon. One night we were starving, so we decided to sneak into the kitchen for a midnight feast.

JANET *(Looking thoughtful)* We made ourselves tea and toast.

DAVID That's right, then we…

JANET Scratched our names inside that cupboard.

DAVID You put a heart with an arrow through it. *(Pause)* We said it was our vow to love each other for ever. *(Pause)* Come and have a look.

JANET *(Looking in cupboard)* It's still here. *(Pause)* We were blissfully happy in those days.

DAVID I'd just finished University and started teaching.

JANET We'd no money, but we managed.

DAVID *(Looking sad)* Over the years, we've drifted apart. *(Aside)* It all started the day your mum moved in.

JANET I've never stopped loving you.

DAVID We take each other for granted nowadays.

JANET Don't forget, we've agreed to make this second honeymoon a new start. This week's going to be a turning point in our marriage.

DAVID Actually things couldn't have worked out better. We've got that sixties day on Friday. We'll pretend we're newly-weds and re-dedicate ourselves to each other.

13

JANET   What a wonderful idea.
DAVID   Let's get a bag of chips and walk down the front.
JANET   But it's pouring with rain.
DAVID   That never used to worry us. We don't do anything on impulse now.
JANET   All right, let's go for it.
DAVID   *(Getting a pen from his pocket)* I'm going to renew our marriage vows.

(David and Janet are writing in the cupboard. Jacks enters from hall he goes into kitchen)

JACK   Is there a problem?
JANET   *(Looking extremely guilty)* No everything's just fine, thanks. *(Pause)* I'd better tell Mum we're going out.
DAVID   I'll get our macs. See you in a sec.

(David and Janet exit to hall, shuffling in an uneasy manner. Jack looks in the cupboard, then shuts the door. The phone rings, Jack goes into dining room and answers it)

JACK   Sea View guest house... Speaking... WHAT!... OH NO!... So it's Toni Clark... Thanks for the tip off. *(Replaces receiver)*

(Jack runs into the kitchen and starts looking around. He runs his finger over the work surfaces. Tina enters from hall and goes into kitchen)

I've just had the *Grand Hotel* on the phone. They said an environmental health officer's coming here.
TINA   It's a bit late for a full English breakfast, isn't it?
JACK   No, Tina. He's not eating here. He's inspecting the kitchens. He'll be poking about in places he's no right to be poking in.
TINA   Oh dear. *(Pause)* So what are we going to do?
JACK   I wonder if they're open to bribes.
TINA   I wouldn't have thought so. *(Pause)* We'd better give the place a spring clean.
JACK   He'll be here any minute. It'll take months to get this place shipshape.
TINA   This reminds me of last week. A policeman was going to book me for speeding. So I gave him an innocent smile, and looked helpless, and guess what? He let me off.
JACK   *(Looking thoughtful)* Hang on a minute, that's it. Tina it's time to flaunt your assets.
TINA   I haven't got any assets. I'm overdrawn.

JACK   Do I have to spell it out? I want you to be nice to him. Take his mind off the job.

TINA   But I'm a respectable girl.

JACK   Come off it, women have been showing a bit of cleavage to get what they wanted since Adam first tasted the fruits of nature. *(Looking serious)* You're our only hope. Just keep him away from the sensitive areas.

TINA   He's certainly not getting anywhere near my sensitive areas.

JACK   No. I mean in the kitchen, behind the cooker, and the worktops.

TINA   I'm not so sure about this. It's not in my job description.

JACK   It could mean promotion, to head waitress.

TINA   *(Getting excited)* Oh. *(Pause)* Hang on, I'm the only waitress here.

JACK   This is an emergency. We've all got to pull together in times of trouble.

TINA   Yeah, but you're not the one he'll be trying to pull.

JACK   *(Grovelling around Tina's feet)* Please, Tina, I'm begging you. *(Pause)* He could close us down. You'll be out of a job.

TINA   *(Reluctantly)* Oh all right, I'll do it.

JACK   *(Kissing Tina)* Thank you, you're a lifesaver. *(Pause)* By the way, his name's Tony.

TINA   I'd better tart myself up if I'm going to be a tart.

JACK   Let's have some soft music, that should get his testosterone flowing.

(Jack and Tina go into dining room. Jack puts on a CD of Elton John singing, "Your Song")

    Right it's over to you, Tina. *(Pause)* I'll make myself scarce.

(Tina and Jack exit to hall. After a few seconds, Marjorie enters from hall and rings service bell. She stands waiting for a second, then goes into the kitchen and starts looking around. Toni Clark enters from hall. She rings service bell, then goes into kitchen)

TONI   Are you the proprietor?

MARJORIE   I beg your pardon?

TONI   My name's Toni Clark. *(Getting out identification card)* I'm an environmental health officer on a routine visit.

MARJORIE   I suggest you get on with it, then. *(Exits to hall)*

TONI   *(Poking around in the kitchen)* Right, let's hope it's not as bad as it looks… Oh dear, it is as bad as it looks. Oh dear. *(Writing down several notes in her book)* Oh dear, this is disgusting... What a mess... absolutely awful... There's serious problems here... Plenty for my report... I can see it's going to be a long day.

(Toni exits to hall. After a few seconds, David enters from hall carrying two macs. He puts them on a table. He checks to see if anyone's about. He then goes into kitchen to cupboard. He opens the door, and gets out his pen and starts writing. Tina enters from hall. She has tarted herself up. She pulls her dress off her shoulders, then goes into kitchen)

TINA   I've been expecting you. *(David jumps away from cupboard)*
DAVID   *(Looking vague)* Have you?
TINA   Yes, you naughty boy, you shouldn't have started without me.
DAVID   *(Looking guilty)* Actually I was just...
TINA   I know exactly what you were doing.
DAVID   That's amazing. It was supposed to be a secret.
TINA   Don't worry. I'm here to make your visit more pleasurable. *(Pause)* Let's have a drink.
DAVID   I haven't really got time at the moment.
TINA   Don't be silly. All work and no play makes Tony a dull boy.
DAVID   Actually it's all work and no play makes Jack a dull boy.
TINA   *(Leading David into dining room)* Oh well, whatever. Come on it's more cosy in here. *(Pause)* Now what do you want to drink?
DAVID   I shouldn't really. *(Pause)* Oh, go on then, I'll have a small orange please.
TINA   One orange coming up.

(Tina pours out two orange drinks. She gets a bottle of gin, and without David seeing, she pours some into one of the drinks. She hands that one to David)

   Cheers.
DAVID   *(Taking a sip)* That's got a bit of a kick.
TINA   *(Getting close to David)* That's because they only pluck the firm oranges. Then they squeeze them, *(sensually)* very tenderly.
DAVID   Really. *(Gulping his orange)*
TINA   What's your taste in music?
DAVID   I'm a bit of a romantic. I like the slow ballads.
TINA   You're like me. After two minutes with Elton John, *(looking into David's eyes)* I'm game for anything.
DAVID   This drink's making me feel light-headed. *(Sits on chair)*

16

TINA   I can't think why. *(Pause)* So what sort of girls do you like? *(Pause)* Intelligent, sporty, pretty?

DAVID   I'm married.

TINA   Just supposing, hypothetically, you could pick a girl. What sort would you go for?

DAVID   This is all very interesting, but I don't think it's the time or place.

(David tries to get out of chair, but Tina pushes him back down)

TINA   I've always gone for the more mature man.

DAVID   *(Gulping down drink)* Have you?

TINA   They've got far more to offer a girl, if you know what I mean.

DAVID   Yes, well it's been nice talking to you.

(David walks to hall exit. Tina pulls him back)

TINA   Don't go yet. We've hardly had a chance to get to know each other. *(Feeling David's muscles)* My, what big biceps you have. *(Pause)* Are you a body builder?

DAVID   Well actually I don't get much time for hobbies.

TINA   Do you enjoy a good workout?

(Tina takes David's glass and without him seeing she fills it with gin)

DAVID   I beg your pardon?

TINA   At the gym, you naughty boy. I can see I'm going to have to watch you.

DAVID   *(Getting embarrassed)* I don't know what you mean.

TINA   So what star sign are you?

DAVID   I'm a Leo.

TINA   I knew it. *(Pause)* I'm a Virgo.

DAVID   I'm very pleased for you. *(Gulping down drink)*

TINA   I'm sorry to mention work, when we're having such a good time, but it'd make such a difference if you'd say our kitchen was up to standard.

DAVID   *(Slurring his words)* It looks perfectly all right to me.

TINA   So you're happy with it?

DAVID   Yes, it seems absolutely fine.

TINA   *(Aside)* I can't believe it's been that easy. *(To David)* Thank you so much.

DAVID   That's all right, think nothing of it.

TINA   *(Getting close to David)* So you'll give us a favourable report?

DAVID   *(Looking vague)* What report are you on about?

17

TINA   (*Getting cross*) Now you've gone and spoilt everything. (*Pause*) Please don't be difficult, Tony.
DAVID   I'm not being difficult.
TINA   We could have some fun if you submitted a good recommendation.
DAVID   I'd like to help, but I don't know…
TINA   Oh, I get it, you want a little taste of what's on offer before signing your life away. (*Pause*) Come here, tiger.

(*Tina grabs David by the chest. She pulls him close and gives him a passionate kiss. Janet enters from hall*)

JANET   Let's go and get those chips, David. (*Pause*) DAVID?

Scene II

As the curtain rises, Jack and Mary are in the kitchen getting breakfast ready.

MARY   It's no good keep blaming Tina. It was your idea.
JACK   I told her to sweeten the health inspector not ravish one of the residents.
MARY   She made a genuine mistake.
JACK   Why didn't she check his credentials?
MARY   From what I've heard, she almost did.
JACK   The reputation of this guest house has been put in jeopardy.
MARY   What about Tina's reputation?
JACK   I'd like to know what happened to that environmental health inspector?

(*Tina enters from hall. She is carrying a cage with a mouse in it. She goes into the kitchen. Jack and Mary do not see the cage*)

MARY   Perhaps he couldn't find us.
JACK   (*Looking hopeful*) With any luck he's been run over by a bus.
TINA   Morning, all.
MARY   Hello, dear. (*Pause*) Jack, you owe Tina an apology.
JACK   I'm sorry Ti… (*Turning round and looking at cage*) Whatever's that?
TINA   His name's Tyson. He's my nephew Andy's pet mouse. I'm looking after him while Andy's on holiday.

MARY *(Getting close to the cage)* Hello, Tyson. Who's a pretty boy then?

JACK Get that mangy thing out of here.

TINA Would you please keep your voice down? Tyson's got a very sensitive disposition.

JACK I don't care if he's a manic depressive, he's not staying here. We may be desperate for guests, but we're certainly not renting rooms to rodents.

TINA Don't worry, I'm taking him to the vet's. He's got an upset tummy.

JACK Are you crazy? A health officer's about to inspect our premises. He'll hardly award a five star rating once he discovers some rodent's been crapping everywhere.

MARY *(Talking to Tyson)* You poor little thing.

TINA *(Putting cage on worktop)* I do hope he's not going to die.

JACK *(To Tina)* Getting back to far more important matters. Your first job this morning'll be to apologise to David Thompson and his wife.

TINA I thought someone would have done that yesterday, on my day off. I'll never be able to face either of them again.

JACK You've no choice, considering you're the front line of our customer service.

(Mary, Tina and Jack continue to work in irate conversation in the kitchen. David and Janet enter from hall. They sit at a table)

JANET And I thought we'd agreed this second honeymoon was going to revitalise our flagging marriage.

DAVID I spent all yesterday telling you she just launched herself at me.

JANET I can't understand why some good looking young female would start making sexual advances to a middle-aged man.

DAVID I can't believe it either. I had to keep on pinching myself to make sure I wasn't dreaming.

JANET I beg your pardon?

DAVID I mean, I've no logical explanation. *(Pause)* Apparently she works here as a waitress.

JANET So what had you got in mind, a threesome over lunch, to spice up the meal and your love life?

DAVID Don't be ridiculous.

JANET All married men are the same. You spend most of your lives fantasising over an extramarital affair with some young sex goddess.

19

DAVID   *(Getting cross)* I've never been unfaithful.

JANET   *(Getting cross)* If you say so.

(David and Janet face away from each other in anger)

MARY   I'm popping to the butcher's, won't be long. *(Goes into dining room)* Morning.

JANET   *(With aggravated expression)* Morning.

MARY   They say it's going to stop raining later.

DAVID   *(With aggravated expression)* That's good.

MARY   *(Goes back into kitchen)* The Thompsons are waiting for their breakfast. *(Pause)* And an explanation. *(Exits to hall)*

JACK   Come on, Tina. It's time to face the music.

TINA   Please don't make me do it, Mr Longthorp.

JACK   Off you go. *(Jack pushes Tina into dining room)* And don't implicate me.

TINA   *(Almost landing on David's lap)* Hello. I owe you both an apology.

(Jack creeps through dining room and exits to hall)

JANET   Don't apologise to my husband. He enjoyed every minute.

TINA   Please let me explain. *(Pause)* You see, *(looking guilty)* I thought your husband was Tony.

JANET   Tony?

TINA   Yes… Um… Tony… Um… Tony Blackburn. He's my mum's idol, she's followed his career from Radio Caroline to Capital Gold. *(Unconvincingly)* Your husband's the spitting image of him.

DAVID   *(Looking pleased)* Do you really think so?

TINA   You're identical. That's why I tried to impress you. I was hoping to persuade you to come home and meet my mum. I'm sorry, I got a bit carried away.

DAVID   So that's why you called me Tony. *(Pause)* But why keep on about the kitchen?

TINA   *(Looking uncertain)* Ah, yes, well, Um… I thought it might help to bring in more guests, if you gave our food preparation department a plug on your radio show.

JANET   And my husband didn't force himself on you?

TINA   No, he was a perfect gentleman. I can assure you, it won't happen again.

DAVID   *(Aside)* What a pity.

JANET   I suppose the story does make sense, apart from any resemblance between my husband and Tony Blackburn.

TINA   Now, *(getting her notepad out)* what would you like to order?

JANET   Tea and toast for two, please.

TINA   Right, I won't be a tick. *(Giving David a nudge)* Tony! *(Goes into kitchen. Makes tea and toast)*

JANET   All right, I'm sorry for doubting you. I should have known better, after thirty-two years of marriage.

DAVID   We can still make this week a new start.

JANET   You're right. *(Janet gets hold of David's hand)* We'll soon bring the sparkle back into our marriage.

MARJORIE   *(Entering from hall)* My bed's as hard as a rock. And those seagulls kept me awake all night.

DAVID   Don't worry. *(Aside)* Now you've arrived, I'm sure they'll all leave.

JANET   So what shall we do today?

MARJORIE   I'm not going far, it's too cold.

JANET   Last time we were here, they had boat trips around the harbour.

MARJORIE   You won't get me on a boat. I can't swim.

DAVID   *(Looking hopeful)* Can't you?

JANET   Let's go for a walk along the front.

(Sara enters from hall. She is arm in arm with Duncan. He gets to their table and collapses in the chair. He looks totally worn out. Sara sits by him)

MARJORIE   Are you joking? It hasn't stopped raining since we got here.

JANET   So what had you got in mind, Mum?

MARJORIE   I've got to get myself some elasticated stockings.

DAVID   *(Aside)* I wonder if they sell elasticated neck collars?

JANET   So we'll do a bit of shopping then?

(Marjorie, Janet and David read newspapers and continue in silent conversation)

SARA   Duncan, I'm not very happy about this.

DUNCAN   I'm doing my best.

SARA   When we agreed I should save myself 'till we were married, I assumed it was because you respected my religious upbringing.

DUNCAN   *(Holding Sara's hand)* That's right, it was.

SARA   *(Pulling her hand away)* I'm beginning to wonder if you had an ulterior motive.

DUNCAN   What are you on about?

SARA   You told me, when it came to the bedroom, you were one of the hottest properties on the market. What you didn't say was that your plumbing needed a major overhaul.

DUNCAN   There isn't a man alive who could keep up with your demands.

SARA   This honeymoon's not fulfilling any of my expectations.

DUNCAN   The wedding vows said, 'Wilt thou love, comfort, honour, and keep her?' There was no mention of working our way through the entire *Kama Sutra* every night.

SARA   *(Getting cross)* Your rugby mates won't be impressed when I tell them you thought the erogenous zones was a pop group.

DUNCAN   *(Getting cross)* Look, I'm all in favour of women having sexual liberty, but you've turned the quest into a crusade.

SARA   I was expecting the earth to move, but you didn't even register on my Richter Scale.

DUNCAN   That's difficult to believe, because I'm still suffering from aftershocks.

SARA   I never realised you wouldn't be up to it.

DUNCAN   *(Shouting)* And I never realised I'd married a nymphomaniac.

(Marjorie, Janet and David all stare. Sara looks embarrassed. Marjorie, Janet and David continue in silent conversation)

SARA   *(Quietly)* We've got to build you up this week. *(Looking at menu)* How about some porridge?

DUNCAN   Please don't mention oats.

(Tina goes into dining room with tea and toast for David and Janet. Jack enters from hall)

JACK   Morning all. *(Jack goes into kitchen)*

TINA   Enjoy your breakfast. *(To Marjorie – shouting)* What would you like to order?

MARJORIE   *(Sarcastically)* After browsing through your extensive menu, I'll just have a coffee.

TINA   One coffee coming up. *(Looks at Duncan, then goes into kitchen)*

JACK   Did you come up with a plausible explanation?

TINA   Yes, and thanks a million for your support. *(Pause)* Fancy doubling your bet?

JACK   You what?

TINA *(Pouring out coffee)* You're so confident your man'll past his virility test, I'm giving you the chance to increase the stakes.

JACK All right, we'll make it forty pounds then.

TINA *(Shaking hands with Jack)* By the way, he's waiting for his breakfast.

JACK And how's the super stud looking?

TINA A bit the worse for wear.

(Tina goes into dining room and gives Marjorie her coffee. Jack goes into dining room and looks at Duncan. Janet writes her holiday postcards)

MARJORIE About time.

(Duncan collapses across the table)

JACK Oh no, he's not capable of doing one press-up, let alone ten. That girl should be forced to carry a government health warning.

TINA *(To Jack)* Fancy making it sixty?

SARA Whatever am I going to do with you, Duncan?

(Sara tries to lift Duncan's head off the table. Jack goes into kitchen. He picks up a dishcloth and soaks it in water)

MARJORIE What's wrong with that boy?

JANET *(Smiling)* It looks as though he's been overdoing it.

MARJORIE How can he, when they're on holiday?

DAVID *(To Marjorie)* Actually, they're on honeymoon. There is a subtle difference.

MARJORIE *(Getting cross)* I'm not stupid. There's no need to get smart with me. *(Walking over to Duncan and poking him with her stick – to Sara)* Is he all right?

SARA He'll be fine, thanks.

MARJORIE If you need any advice, *(sarcastically and looking at David)* you'd better ask the marriage guidance counsellor over there.

SARA Marriage guidance counsellor? Actually that's just what I need. *(Shouting over to David)* Excuse me. *(Pause)* Perhaps we could have a chat sometime.

JANET What was that all about?

DAVID *(Looking vague)* I've absolutely no idea.

(Jack goes into dining room and drapes the wet dishcloth over Duncan's head)

SARA   *(To Jack and Tina)* Would you mind giving me a hand? I'll take him back to bed.

JACK   He'll be like a lamb to the slaughter. *(To Sara)* You've got to show him some mercy. You could do the poor lad some serious damage.

(Tina and Jack arm Duncan through hall exit. The wet dishcloth is draped over his head. Sara follows them out)

MARJORIE   This coffee tastes like dishwater. I can't drink it.

JANET   We'll get a coffee in town. *(Pause)* Let's get our shopping bags. Are you coming, David?

DAVID   I'm finishing my toast first.

MARJORIE   I can't see how you can eat that burnt offering.

JANET   Don't be long, dear, we'll wait for you upstairs.

(Marjorie and Janet exit to hall. After a few seconds, Amina enters from hall. She sits at a spare table reading a paper. She looks at David)

AMINA   Hello, Mr Thompson.

DAVID   *(Looking vague)* I'm sorry, do I know you?

AMINA   Amina Betnay. *(Pause)* Perhaps if I called you sir, it might help.

DAVID   *(Looking thoughtful)* Amina Betnay?

AMINA   Go back nearly thirty years – Hyde Park Comprehensive School – a bespectacled teenager, enjoying the delights of severe acne.

DAVID   That narrows it down to half the pupils I've taught.

AMINA   My biological clock had just struck, and my hormones were working overtime.

DAVID   The advent of adolescence. When the school bike shed takes on a whole new meaning.

AMINA   I had a desperate crush on a teacher called Mr Thompson.

DAVID   Oh dear, this is getting a bit too close for comfort.

AMINA   I used to hang about after class, hoping to see you.

DAVID   Now that was unusual. Most pupils treated the end of lesson bell as a fire alarm.

AMINA   You always helped me when I found the work too difficult.

DAVID   Amina Betnay. *(Thinking)* Yes, I do remember. *(With desire)* You've certainly changed. *(David and Amina shake hands)* So what are you doing now?

AMINA   I'm a journalist for a national paper.

DAVID   Congratulations; you've done well.

AMINA Thanks to your steadfast efforts. You were the best teacher in the school. *(Pause)* I meant it when I said I had a crush on you.

DAVID *(Glibly)* So my wife's got a bit of competition?

AMINA *(Looking into David's eyes)* She's a very lucky woman.

DAVID *(Getting embarrassed)* Yes, well, I think it's time I went. I've been summoned to go shopping with mother-in-law. *(Pause)* Nice to meet you again.

AMINA See you soon.

(David exits to hall. Amina stares into space for a few seconds, she smiles then exits to hall. Tina enters from hall. She looks at the tables which need clearing and throws her hands forward in an apathetic gesture)

TINA *(Shouting)* It's all right, Tyson, Mummy's here. *(Tina goes into kitchen and picks up cage)* Tyson, where are you? *(Tina spots the cage door is open)* Oh no, someone's left the door open and he's got out. *(Tina frantically looks around kitchen)* Tyson, Tyson.

(Toni Clark enters from hall carrying a briefcase. She rings the service bell. Tina runs into dining room)

(Getting frustrated) Yes, can I help you?

TONI I'd like to see the proprietor please.

TINA Oh right. Look, could you hang on a sec? I've got a major crisis in the kitchen.

TONI *(Aside)* You've taken the words right out of my mouth.

TINA *(Frantically)* Tyson's gone walkabout. *(Pause)* One minute he was in his cage, and the next he'd disappeared.

TONI So who's Tyson?

TINA A psychologically unstable mouse. I kept him in the kitchen, but someone's left his cage door open. *(In desperation)* Would you help me look for him?

TONI Well, I suppose I could give you a hand. *(Aside)* It'll give me another chance to look around.

TINA *(Tina and Toni go into kitchen)* He's got to be here somewhere. Let's try the cupboards first. *(Tina and Toni look in all the cupboards)* Tyson come to Mummy. Don't be frightened.

TONI None of this high protein food's stored in temperature controlled conditions.

TINA Let's hope he doesn't eat any. *(Pause)* I'm not sure how long it's been there. *(Shouting)* Tyson, where are you?

TONI You seem to mix the cooked and uncooked foods together.

25

TINA   I know, it gets very confusing at times.

TONI   *(Looking at food)* There isn't any labelling on these chicken breasts. They should all have use-by dates marked on them.

TINA   *(Getting cross)* Look, I don't wish to appear ungrateful. But could we please concentrate on finding Tyson?

TONI   *(Looking around kitchen)* Just as a point of interest, how do you tell when food's past it's use-by date?

TINA   Jack usually makes that decision. He says you can always smell if something's off.

TONI   And who's Jack? The owner of the mouse?

TINA   No, he's the proprietor of this guest house.

TONI   He's very lucky having such a sensitive nose. Most of us have to rely on more scientific methods.

TINA   *(Speaking with authority)* As Jack says – we've all got to eat some bacteria. It keeps our immune system on its toes. *(Pause)* His theory is, we're all too squeaky clean nowadays.

TONI   So what does your brochure say – we offer sea, sun and salmonella?

TINA   Let's just say we've not killed off anybody, *(pause)* yet.

TONI   *(Aside)* I'd say your guests have been very lucky. *(To Tina)* Doesn't it worry you that you've got a mouse at large in a kitchen full of food?

TINA   Of course it does. *(Pause)* If I don't find him, my nephew'll kill me.

TONI   *(Aside)* That's assuming the germs in here don't finish you off first.

TINA   *(Lifting the lid on a large saucepan of mincemeat)* I hope he's not in this mincemeat. *(Pause)* I can't see any footprints.

TONI   *(Looking into saucepan)* Let's hope he's not tried it, then decided to move on.

TINA   *(Smelling mincemeat)* I daren't risk it. *(Jack enters from hall)*

TONI   So you'll throw the mincemeat away?

TINA   No, I'll boil it for an extra ten minutes, just in case he's left any little presents. *(Jack goes into kitchen)* Thank goodness you're here. Tyson's gone walkabout.

JACK   I told you to keep that wretched thing locked up.

TINA   I've no idea where he is. *(Pause)* Fortunately this nice lady's offered to help me look. This is Mr Longthorp, I'm sorry I don't know your name.

TONI   It's Toni Clark.

JACK   Toni Clark?

26

TONI   Yes, I've been wanting to meet you, Mr Longthorpe. I'm your local Environmental Health Inspector.

(Jack looks horrified)

Scene III

As the curtain rises, Jack and Mary are in the kitchen preparing the evening meal.

JACK   Have you seen the yellow pages? I'm looking for an estate agent, and flogging this place off.

MARY   And what's brought about this drastic decision?

JACK   Our bookings have hit rock bottom. We've got an environmental health inspector trying to close us down. And if that's not enough, we've been lumbered with the holidaymaker from hell.

MARY   We've ploughed our life savings into this guest house.

JACK   Don't you think I know that? Let's just say I'd rather jump before I'm pushed.

MARY   That health inspector was very reasonable once we'd explained about Tyson.

JACK   Reasonable? She's sent a twenty page ultimatum listing her demands or she's going to close us down.

MARY   She's given us 'til Saturday to sort things out.

JACK   I still can't understand why she was unresponsive to my charm.

MARY   *(Sarcastically)* It's probably because like most of the food in this kitchen, you're past your sell-by date.

JACK   I'm getting a job and letting someone else have all this hassle.

MARY   And what job have you got in mind?

JACK   I've no idea. *(Looking thoughtful)* I'm too old to be a copper, too young to work at B and Q, and too knackered to be a night porter. *(Pause)* My life's in a mess.

TINA   *(Enters from hall. Goes into kitchen – crying)* I didn't sleep a wink last night.

JACK   Join the club.

TINA   Whatever are we going to do?

MARY   Jack's been on about selling the place.

27

TINA *(Stops crying)* No, I meant what are we going to do about Tyson? He's probably gasping his last breath, with his little feet flapping in the air.

JACK My whole empire's about to collapse before I've even had a chance to float it on the stock exchange, and you're worried about some flea-infested mouse.

TINA Haven't you got a heart?

JACK Of course I have, but it stops short of getting upset over some elusive vermin. *(Pause)* That rodent's caused me a lot of grief.

(David enters from hall. He sits in dining room and reads a newspaper)

TINA We should have organised a search party.

MARY Perhaps we should check he's not in the bedrooms.

JACK You're right. I'll give you a hand.

TINA I'll be there in a minute.

(Jack and Mary exit to hall. Tina goes into dining room)

Oh, David you've got to help me.

DAVID Please don't start all that again. I've only just convinced my wife our last meeting was innocent.

TINA No you don't understand, I've lost my nephew's mouse. *(Pause)* I was taking him to the vet's, but he escaped.

DAVID Oh I see. *(Pause)* He won't have gone far. He'll turn up when he's ready.

TINA I do hope you're right. I've been so worried.

DAVID He's probably having the time of his life. Now, you cheer up.

TINA Thank you. It's nice to meet a man who's caring and kind. *(Getting close)* Especially one who looks like Tony Blackburn.

(Tina exits to hall. Janet and Marjorie enter from hall and sit by David)

DAVID Did you enjoy your walk?

MARJORIE Is that supposed to be a joke? The place is full of screaming kids. They're all running wild on the beach.

DAVID That's what youngsters do on holiday. It's called having fun.

MARJORIE In my day children were seen and not heard. *(To Janet)* Did you see that group of teenagers hanging about on the street corner? One of the girls had a love bite on her neck. It was disgusting.

DAVID   *(Aside – to Janet)* I seem to remember you gave me a couple of love bites on our honeymoon.

MARJORIE   What are you muttering about?

JANET   *(Unconvincingly)* David said we visited a couple of lovely sights on our honeymoon. *(Aside – to David)* Don't you dare say another word.

MARJORIE   This country's going to the dogs. The churches are empty. The jails are full. It's not the monarchy that rules, it's yob culture. *(Pause)* The trouble is parents don't take their responsibilities seriously nowadays. *(Looking at Janet)* I would have loved more children, but I had such a difficult pregnancy with you.

DAVID   *(Aside)* Not the nine months of hell again, please.

MARJORIE   I suffered nine months of hell. Morning sickness, heartburn, craving for foods I'd never even heard of. And if that wasn't enough, *(looking at Janet)* you were up every night for the first three years.

DAVID   *(Aside)* It's almost sleep deprivation time.

MARJORIE   My doctor said he'd never seen such a severe case of sleep deprivation. You cried incessantly.

JANET   I'm so sorry, Mum.

(Jack enters from hall)

MARJORIE   I'm not blaming you dear. It's what parenting's all about. All we ask in return is that our children show appreciation for all the sacrifices we've made.

JACK   Afternoon all.

MARJORIE   *(To Jack)* You had a health inspector round on Saturday. I told her to check out the kitchens thoroughly.

JACK   *(Getting cross)* Thanks a million.

MARJORIE   *(Looking smug)* So how many serious problems did she find?

JACK   Actually, we've been given a clean bill of health. *(Goes into the kitchen and bangs the frying pan on the work-top. He makes himself busy tidying up)*

MARJORIE   I don't believe that for one minute. *(Pause)* Since I've been here my stomach's been all over the place. Why they wouldn't send a doctor round here to check me over, I'll never know.

JANET   You should have gone to the surgery, Mum. Like they told you to.

MARJORIE   What, and sit in a waiting room full of sick people? You go in with a migraine and leave with the mumps. *(Pause)* We should have had private health care.

JANET   So what shall we do now? *(Everyone sits in silence for a few seconds)* We are allowed to have fun, we're on holiday.

MARJORIE   *(Aside)* It wasn't my idea to come here.

JANET   I've got it, let's go and watch the band playing.

(Tina enters from hall and goes into kitchen)

MARJORIE   It's hardly the highlight of the week. Still, I suppose it's better than sitting in this morgue.

JANET   How about you, David?

DAVID   I'm happy here, thanks.

JANET   *(Glaring at David)* Right, so we'll see you a bit later.

(Janet and Marjorie exit to hall. David reads a newspaper)

JACK   *(To Tina)* You're not to mention that mouse to our guests.

TINA   Why not? The more people who know, the better our chance of finding Tyson.

JACK   That old battle-axe Braithwaite's just looking for any excuse to cause trouble. The minute she gets wheeze there's a mouse on the loose she'll go for my jugular.

TINA   So what do I tell my nephew when he phones about Tyson?

JACK   Tell him he'll be washing up here for the next six months to compensate for all the grief that rodent's caused me. *(Pause)* By the way I've decided to let you off our bet.

TINA   Sorry?

JACK   I'd feel guilty about taking your money when my man's done his ten press-ups.

TINA   There's no way I'm calling it off. He's clapped out.

JACK   All right, but don't come crying to me when I've taken all your money. *(Pause)* We'd better go and check the lounge is clean. I don't want old Braithwaite finding a speck of dust on the telly.

TINA   Okay. *(Goes into dining room – aside to David)*
    Please don't say anything about the mouse.

DAVID   *(Looking out from behind his newspaper)* Sorry?

(Jack goes into dining room unseen by Tina)

TINA   Don't mention the mouse.

DAVID   Mouse?

JACK   What are you two talking about?

TINA   *(To David)* So you'd like a moose for desert. Right I'll jot that down, no problem. *(Exits to hall)*

JACK   *(Quietly)* Any idea where I could get bromide from?

DAVID   I beg your pardon?

JACK   They used to give it to the troops in the last war. It was to calm their libido down. They slipped it into the tea.

DAVID   I've no idea.

JACK   Oh, well, not to worry. *(Pause)* Must get on.

(Jack exits to hall and David reads his newspaper. Amina enters from hall carrying a shopping bag. She sits by David)

AMINA   Hi.

DAVID   Hello, enjoying your holiday?

AMINA   It's super, thanks.

DAVID   So what have you been doing since you left Hyde Park School?

AMINA   After leaving university, I looked for a job in the national press. I was naive enough to think it would be easy. But it's still a man's world out there.

DAVID   Things are changing.

AMINA   That's true, but you're still up against men who think a woman's only role in society is to pop out to the shops or pop out babies.

DAVID   Still, you've made it. *(Pause)* Did you ever marry?

AMINA   No, I've had a string of unsuccessful relationships, but never found that special person.

DAVID   I'm sure he'll turn up one day.

AMINA   *(Looking into David's eyes)* Do you know, I think you could be right. *(Pause)* So what have you been doing?

DAVID   I'm still teaching English. Our kids have moved out and the mother-in-law's moved in. *(Pause)* It's depressing when you can sum up your whole life in a couple of sentences.

AMINA   I hope you won't be offended but I've brought you a small present.

DAVID   A present. Why ever would you do that?

AMINA   I wanted to say thank you for all you did for me at school. *(Handing over a CD)* It's nothing much.

DAVID   What a lovely thought. *(Opens wrapping and looks at CD)* It's Barry White. He's made some great tracks.

AMINA   I chose this one especially for you. *(Taking CD from David)* The message is in the words.

31

(Amina plays CD of Barry White singing My First, My Last, My Everything. She returns and sits by David. They listen to the first few seconds of the CD. Sara enters from hall)

SARA   *(To David)* I wonder if I could have a word with you in private?
DAVID   Um, yes certainly.
AMINA   I've got a couple of phone calls to make. I'll see you in a minute, David.

(Sara sits at a table. Amina exits to hall. David removes his CD from player and sits by Sara)

DAVID   It's turned out nice, now.
SARA   Yes, much better.
DAVID   Where's your husband, has he gone for a swim?
SARA   *(Looking disgusted)* No, he's gone to bed, for another sleep.
DAVID   We had our honeymoon here thirty-two years ago. *(Looking thoughtful)* They were some of the happiest days of my life. That's why we decided to come back for a second visit. It's been wonderful, reliving all those precious memories.
SARA   *(Starting to cry)* I wanted my honeymoon to be perfect, but everything's going wrong.
DAVID   Don't cry. I'm sure things'll improve, especially now the weather's brightened up. *(Handing Sara a handkerchief)*
SARA   It's not the weather, it's Duncan.
DAVID   Duncan?
SARA   Yes, he's not the man I thought he was. I don't even think we're compatible.
DAVID   He seems like a real nice lad to me.
SARA   *(Still crying)* He's absolutely gorgeous. I just love him to bits.
DAVID   I don't understand. If you love him, what's the…?
SARA   I didn't want to burden you with my troubles, especially when you're on holiday. But when your mother-in-law said you were in the job, it seemed too good an opportunity to miss.
DAVID   So it's something to do with teaching?
SARA   *(Looking vague)* Teaching? No it's a bit more personal than that. *(Pause)* I just want your professional advice. *(Sara stops crying)* Promise me this won't go any further.
DAVID   *(Patting Sara's hand)* On my mother-in-law's life.
SARA   Actually it's a bit delicate. *(Pause)* My parents are very religious, and I was brought up to have strong moral principles.
DAVID   That's refreshing to hear.

32

SARA   Duncan was understanding when I said we should wait until our marriage before we, well, you know…

DAVID   *(Walking around the room – looking awkward)* I think I'm getting the picture.

SARA   I know it's unusual nowadays, but I thought it would make it more special.

DAVID   So what's the problem?

SARA   Duncan lacks any self-control.

DAVID   What do you mean, he loses his temper?

SARA   No, I'm talking about in the bedroom.

DAVID   So what are you saying, he snores?

SARA   How can I put this. *(Pause)* By the time I've got in the starting blocks, he's passed the winning post. And then I have to wait at least five minutes before he's ready to begin the next race. *(Pause)* He thinks that foreplay's a computer game.

DAVID   Good grief! You should be talking to the marriage guidance people.

SARA   But I thought I was. Your mother-in-law said you were in the job.

DAVID   *(Sitting by Sara)* She was being her usual sarcastic self. *(Pause)* I'm a school teacher, but if you want a totally unprofessional opinion, I'd say you're worrying unnecessarily. Making love is ten per cent friction and ninety per cent fantasy. He'll soon sort himself out. And what's more, it's fun practising.

SARA   You're talking a lot of sense.

(Jack enters from hall, unseen by Sara or David)

It's nice to meet a man with experience on lovemaking. Thank you. *(Sara kisses David. Jack stares in disbelief. Sara spots Jack)* Oh, hello. *(Pause)* See you later, David. *(Sara notices that the top button on her blouse is undone. She does it up, then exits to hall)*

JACK   I wondered how you kept your marriage alive for all those years. Just be careful with that girl, she's dynamite.

DAVID   I didn't realise you could hear. Please don't say anything.

JACK   Don't worry about me. This is brilliant news. You've just shortened my odds of winning.

DAVID   *(Looking vague)* Winning what?

(Jack goes into the kitchen. David reads a paper. Tina enters from hall and goes into kitchen)

JACK   I'm willing to increase our bet to fifty pounds.

TINA   You've certainly changed your tune. Two minutes ago you wanted to call it off.
JACK   If you don't want some extra cash, that's fine by…
TINA   Oh, go on then, we'll make it fifty.

(Janet and Marjorie enter from hall. Marjorie is having a job to walk and is holding onto Janet)

DAVID   That was quick.
JANET   They had to cancel the concert.
MARJORIE   Someone's stolen all their instruments. *(Hobbles across to the service bell and rings it)*
JACK   You go, Tina, I recognise Marjorie Braithwaite's ring.
TINA   *(Goes into dining room)* Can I help?
MARJORIE   Two teas, and I'll have some cake.
TINA   Right, madam, won't be a moment.
MARJORIE   And make sure the cake's fresh.

(Tina goes into kitchen and continues in silent conversation with Jack)

JANET   Sit down and rest, Mum. It'll help ease your arthritis.
MARJORIE   We should have gone to the Mediterranean. Why we had to come to this God-forsaken place I'll never know.
DAVID   *(Aside)* You could always go home.
MARJORIE   *(Marjorie tries to sit down)* Ah… You wait till you get to my age. *(Sits in chair)* Then you'll realise what you have to put up with.
DAVID   I already know. You give me a progress report every two minutes.
MARJORIE   *(To Janet)* Are you going to let him talk to me like that?
JANET   David, I think you should apologise to Mummy. That was uncalled-for.
DAVID   Your mum should have written the hypochondriac's handbook. *(Pause)* There's not a part of her body which hasn't been afflicted by some mythical ailment. *(Aside)* With the exception of her mouth.
MARJORIE   *(To Janet)* I spent my whole life making sacrifices for you, and this is how I'm treated.
DAVID   *(Aside)* Oh no, not the bleeding hearts and flowers routine again.

(Janet, David and Marjorie continue in aggravated silent conversation. Mary enters from hall and goes into kitchen)

MARY   He's not in the bedroom.

TINA   *(Getting upset)* I'm never going to see my little Tyson again.

MARY   Now come on cheer up. *(Pause)* Don't forget we've got the sixties day tomorrow.

JACK   It hardly seems worth bothering with. The way things are going, we'll soon be closed.

MARY   For goodness sake, change the record.

TINA   Talking of records, my mum's lending me some of her sixties hits.

(Duncan enters from the hall. He sits at a table and reads a large copy of the Kama Sutra)

MARY   That's very kind of her. *(Pause)* I've already sorted out my dress. *(To Jack)* You've still got a pair of those old flare trousers, haven't you?

TINA   *(Looking at Jacks stomach)* They'll need letting out.

JACK   Do you mind?

TINA   *(Goes into dining room, carrying two teas and a plate of cakes)* Two teas and a selection of cakes. *(Hands Janet her tea)*

JANET   Thank you.

TINA   *(To Marjorie)* Tea. *(Hands Marjorie her tea)* And some fresh cakes.

MARJORIE   *(Takes a cake and screams)* Ah... Ah... Ah...

TINA   Whatever's wrong? It's only a chocolate sponge.

(Marjorie runs around the dining room. There is no sign of her arthritis)

MARJORIE   Ah... Ah...

TINA   *(Looking at cakes)* Tyson. You naughty boy. Mummy's been worried about you.

MARJORIE   Get that wretched rat away from me.

DUNCAN   *(Shouting)* Rat!

(Tina strokes Tyson, Duncan jumps onto a chair)

TINA   *(Indignantly)* It's not a rat, it's a pedigree mouse. *(Pause)* Don't be frightened, Tyson, no one's going to hurt you.

(Jack and Mary run into dining room)

JACK   What's going on in here?

TINA   Tyson's come home. Look he's tucking into the Swiss roll. *(Pause)* Come here, darling. *(Goes to pick up Tyson, but he jumps off the plate onto the floor)*

35

Oh no, he's jumped off the plate. He could have broken his little neck.

(Duncan jumps off chair and runs through hall exit)

JACK   Don't mess about, grab him.

(Marjorie is still running around the room. Tyson exits to hall)

MARY   *(Pointing to hall exit)* There he goes, into the hall.
TINA   We've got to catch him. Come on, everyone.

(Tina, Jack and Mary exit to hall)

MARJORIE   I don't feel very well. *(Collapses over a chair and starts gasping for breath)*
DAVID   At least it's cured your arthritis.
JANET   *(Janet takes Marjorie's tea from table and gives her the cup)* Have a sip of tea, Mum, you'll soon feel better.
MARJORIE   I could have irreversible heart damage, and recurring nightmares.
DAVID   *(Aside)* The mouse is more likely to have nightmares.
MARJORIE   My whole body's shaking. I'm going to have a lie-down.
JANET   I'll come with you.
MARJORIE   No, you stay with your husband. *(With self-pity)* I don't want to be a burden to anyone. *(Hobbles through hall exit)*
JANET   *(Getting cross)* I hope you're happy now.
DAVID   And what's that supposed to mean?
JANET   My mother's a frail old lady, and you've spent this entire holiday bullying her.
DAVID   *(Getting cross)* Even the most hardened criminal wouldn't be able to intimidate your mum. *(Pause)* She moved in with us for one week, ten years ago. I'd say she's outstayed her welcome.
JANET   Mummy doesn't interfere.
DAVID   Are you joking? *(Pause)* The only place I'm ever alone with you is in bed. It wouldn't surprise me to see your mum's head popping out from under the sheets one night.
JANET   So everything's my mother's fault?
DAVID   We were soulmates until she turned our home into a jail. Now we're cell mates. *(Pause)* We've got to do something before it's too late. That's assuming you want to save our marriage.
JANET   I haven't got the time for all this now. *(Pause)* I'm going to make sure she's all right.
DAVID   That's right, go to Mummy.

(Janet exits to hall. David looks thoughtful. After a few seconds, Amina enters from hall)

AMINA   Hi.

DAVID   Thanks for the CD, it was very kind of you.

AMINA   It was my pleasure. *(Pause)* I fancy a coffee. *(Rings service bell)*

DAVID   You won't get any response. Everyone's chasing a mouse, at the moment. It almost bit my mother-in-law.

AMINA   That could have been serious.

DAVID   You're right, the mouse could have finished up with blood poisoning.

AMINA   Let's hope they catch it.

(Tyson enters from hall and runs into kitchen)

DAVID   Yes, I'd like to thank it personally.

(Tina, Jack and Mary enter from hall)

TINA   *(Pointing to kitchen)* He's gone into the kitchen.

(Tina, Jack and Mary run into kitchen)

MARY   Come here, darling, we're not going to hurt you.

JACK   No of course we're not.

(Tina and Jack look in the cupboards)

TINA   *(Shouting)* Mummy's got a nice piece of cheese for you.

(Tyson runs through dining room and exits to hall)

MARY   He's heading back into the hall.

TINA   He must be feeling better. He's got much more energy now.

AMINA   Is there any chance of a coffee…?

(Tina, Jack and Mary exit to hall)

It looks as though we'll have to make our own. *(Pause)* Do you want a cup?

DAVID   I'd love one.

AMINA   I suggest we help ourselves, then.

(Amina and David go into kitchen. Amina puts the kettle on and searches around for coffee)

Where's the coffee? *(Finds coffee)* Ah, here it is. *(Puts coffee into cups)*

DAVID   I can't believe it's been nearly thirty years since I taught you. *(Looking thoughtful)* Where's my life gone?

AMINA   It's a bad sign when you start looking back.

DAVID   When you're young everything seems black and white, but with age comes the grey area.

AMINA   That sounds very philosophical.

DAVID   It's just a middle-aged man taking stock of life, and trying to remember what it was like when he felt alive.

AMINA   We women have our problems as well. *(Pause)* The body sags. The smile which used to entice male drivers to allow me out of a junction doesn't work any more. I can sit there for hours waiting for a gap.

DAVID   I don't believe it. You're very attractive.

AMINA   You should be careful, telling a doting pupil things like that.

DAVID   You're no longer my pupil. I'm sure all those feelings have disappeared.

AMINA   How wrong you are. *(Getting close to David)* The minute I set eyes on you again, it was as though …

DAVID   I think it's time for that coffee.

AMINA   Yes, you're probably right. *(Pours out two coffees and gives one to David)*

DAVID   Thank you. *(Knocks his head on an open cupboard door)* Ouch, damn. I didn't see that door.

AMINA   Are you all right? Is it bleeding?

DAVID   *(Rubbing his head)* It hurts like hell.

AMINA   You poor thing. Let me have a look. *(Examines David's head)* Come here, I'll kiss it better.

(Amina kisses David's forehead, leaving a big kiss mark in the centre of it)

DAVID   *(Jokingly)* It still hurts. *(Pause)* I think I need a bit more of your therapy.

(David and Amina make eye contact. They go into a passionate kiss. Sara enters from hall and rings service bell. Amina and David break off the kiss)

You stay here, I'll see who it is. *(Goes into dining room)*

SARA   I'm glad you're here, I just wanted to say how much I appreciated your advice.

DAVID   *(Looking confused)* Sorry?

(David is in a dazed state. He still has a large kiss mark in the centre of his forehead. Sara does not notice it)

SARA   You must have thought I was stupid, pouring out my love life. *(Pause)* Are you all right?

DAVID   *(Still in a dazed state)* Yes, I've just been... Um... Having a... ki... coffee.

SARA   I think I'll get myself a coffee.

(Sara walks towards kitchen, David pulls her back)

DAVID   No you can't. I mean, I'll get it for you. *(Runs into kitchen and pours out a coffee. Amina grabs him)*

AMINA   *(Whispering)* I've been missing you. *(Pause)* How's the head?

DAVID   Still sore.

(Amina gives David a second kiss mark on his forehead)

　　　I'd better take this coffee in.

AMINA   Don't be long.

(David goes into dining room with coffee and hands it to Sara. She doesn't notice the two kiss marks. Meanwhile Amina applies more lipstick to her lips)

DAVID   Here you are.

SARA   Thanks. You've been so kind and understanding. *(Pause)* I've never been able to talk to my own dad.

DAVID   I'm pleased I was able to help.

SARA   *(Taking a sip of coffee)* Actually, I take sugar in coffee. I'll get some.

DAVID   *(Grabbing Sara's coffee)* No, leave it to me. *(Runs into kitchen and puts sugar in coffee)* All this is doing my head in.

AMINA   Come here, let me ease the tension.

(Amina gives David a third kiss mark on his forehead. David takes coffee into dining room and gives it to Sara. He slumps into a chair. Sara spots the three kiss marks)

SARA   You'd better tell your wife to buy kiss-proof lipstick.

DAVID   I beg your pardon?

SARA   Lipstick, you've got it all over your forehead. Stay there, I'll wipe it off.

(Sara gets a tissue. She bends over David and is just about to wipe off lipstick when Janet enters from hall)

JANET   I shouldn't have gone off like…
DAVID   Oh, hello, dear.

(David tries to stand up but pulls Sara down so she finishes up sitting on his lap)

JANET   *(Looking at three kiss marks on forehead)* So what's your mission this week, to work your way through all the females in alphabetical order?

(Jack enters from hall)

SARA   *(To Janet)* You should be pleased. I'm saving you a job. *(Wipes off lipstick marks)*
JANET   *(Looking horrified)* You what?
JACK   *(Aside to David)* I told you to be discreet with your affairs. Now the pressure's back on my man.
DUNCAN   *(Entering from hall)* Sara, what are you doing?
SARA   I was only getting them off, for David.
JANET   Good grief, he's turned this guest house into his harem.
JACK   *(Aside)* He's certainly bitten off more than he can chew with that girl.
DUNCAN   Could someone tell me what's going on?
SARA   *(Standing by Duncan)* If you'd all give me a chance I'll explain, you see …
JANET   Let me guess. *(Sarcastically – to Sara)* You think my husband looks like Chris Evans, and your parents want to meet him. *(Aside – to David)* My mother was right. You're nothing but a philandering waste of space. *(Hits David round the head)* Our marriage is over.

(David looks bemused)

BLACKOUT

ACT II

Scene I

As the curtain rises, Mary, Jack, David, and Janet are sitting down watching Tina doing the twist to Brian Pool and the Tremeloes singing 'Do you love me?' Everyone is wearing sixties clothes. There are lots of sixties pop group posters around the room. The music fades down low. Alternatively, Mary, Jack, David, Janet and Tina could come off stage and jive with members of the audience. The music fades down low.

JACK   Time for nibbles.

(Tina and Mary take round the trays of nibbles. Jack starts looking through some sixties CDs)

JANET   You're very quiet, David. *(Pause)* Are you all right?

DAVID   Well, after the grilling you gave me yesterday, I'm not sure.

JANET   I've said I'm sorry. It's just that every time I turn my back you start fondling some frustrated female.

DAVID   *(Looking guilty)* I admit it looked like lipstick, but I can assure you it was red ink from a felt tip pen. *(Pause)* I wanted to renew our wedding vows. So I got a pen, but hadn't noticed it was leaking onto my fingers. *(Pause)* As I was scratching my brains, thinking what to write, I inadvertently transferred red ink all over my forehead.

JANET   So why was Sara sitting on your lap?

DAVID   She came into the room, spotted the red ink and offered to clean me up.

JANET   I suppose it makes sense. I mean, let's face facts, Sara's young enough to be your daughter.

DAVID   *(Indignantly)* Exactly, I'm hardly going to start flirting with some child bride.

JANET   Just tell me one thing. Why do men find the sight of a slender, firm, female body so irresistible?

DAVID   I wouldn't know, dear. *(Aside)* It's been so long since I've seen one.

41

JANET   All right. I've made a complete fool of myself again.
DAVID   And I thought we were going to make a new start this week.
JANET   *(Holding David's hand)* It's not too late. *(Pause)* Dressed in this sixties gear, I feel like we've moved back in time to those wonderful days of our honeymoon.

(Marjorie enters from hall. She is wearing a flower power outfit and a wig. She looks ridiculous)

MARJORIE   I don't know why you made me wear this ridiculous get up.
JANET   We've all got to enter into the spirit of the occasion, Mum.

(Marjorie sits at the table with Janet and David)

JACK   *(Shouting)* If anyone's got a sixties favourite, let me know.
DAVID   *(To Janet)* Can you remember, on our honeymoon there was a song we kept hearing throughout the week?
JANET   It was sung by Gerry and the Pacemakers. *(Lovingly)* We called it our special tune.
DAVID   Whenever I hear it, all those wonderful memories return.
JANET   It always gives me a tingling sensation at the back of my neck.
MARJORIE   That'll be the start of arthritis. You'll be crippled by the time you reach my age.

(Tina and Mary finish handing round the nibbles, then go into the kitchen and start cleaning the work surfaces)

JANET   On our last night, we went to that dance at the end of the pier, and got them to play our tune.
DAVID   By the time we left, it was the early hours of the morning.
JANET   *(Holding David's hand – romantically)* We walked along the beach. The moon was glistening on the sea. Everything was so peaceful. And for one magical moment, the world seemed perfect.
MARJORIE   It's a wonder you didn't get mugged, wandering about at that time in the morning.
DAVID   I'm going to see if he's got our record. *(Walking over to Jack)*
MARJORIE   Oh no, he's not going to start that organ-grinder off again.

(Marjorie and Janet continue in silent conversation. Jack and David sort through CDs)

TINA   Well, today's certainly been a success.

MARY   Jack's been more like his old self. I've not seen him so happy in years.

TINA   He won't be happy when I've taken his fifty quid.

MARY   I wonder where Sara and Duncan are?

TINA   Let's hope they're in bed. With any luck she'll be draining the last drop of energy from him. *(Pause)* I'm just praying he'll be too knackered to do ten press-ups. I'm skint.

(Tina and Mary continue in silent conversation)

JANET   Have you enjoyed your holiday, Mum?

MARJORIE   Is that supposed to be a joke? Your husband's been extremely rude to me, all week. *(Eating sausage roll)*

JANET   You're being over sensitive. *(Pause)* Look if you're that worried, I'll get him to apologise.

MARJORIE   I'll believe that when I hear it. *(Pause)* These sausage rolls are as hard as bullets.

(Jack goes into kitchen and continues in silent conversation with Tina and Mary. David walks back over to Janet and Marjorie)

DAVID   *(Looking pleased)* He's got it, and he's going to play it.

JANET   *(To David)* You owe Mum an apology.

DAVID   Whatever for?

MARJORIE   I knew he wouldn't do it.

JANET   Look, David, you've got to admit you've been a bit off with Mother this week. Just tell her you didn't mean anything.

DAVID   *(Getting cross)* I'm very sorry...

JANET   Thank you David. *(Pause)* All right, Mum? Now everyone's happy.

DAVID   No, please let me finish. *(To Marjorie)* I'm very sorry that for the past ten years I've let you come between Janet and me.

JANET   David.

DAVID   I'm very sorry that I've let you play us off against each other and ruin a perfectly good marriage.

JANET   David.

DAVID   I'm very sorry that I didn't lock all the doors and windows when I heard you were on your way.

JANET   David.

MARJORIE   I don't know what to say. *(Taking a large bite of sausage roll)*

DAVID   *(Shouting)* I know what I'd like to say. Pis...

JANET   DAVID!

43

(David sits down. Marjorie starts choking on her sausage roll)

MARJORIE   *(Choking)* Ah… Ah…
JANET   Mother, whatever's up?
MARJORIE   Ah… Ah…
JANET   David didn't mean it. He was only having a little joke.
MARJORIE   Ah… Ah… *(Pointing to her mouth)*
DAVID   *(Looking across to Marjorie)* Oh no, she's got something stuck in her throat.

(Janet jumps up and starts hitting Marjorie on her back)

MARJORIE   Ah… Ah… *(Unable to get her breath)*
JANET   *(Shouting)* Would someone please help?

(Marjorie jumps out of her chair and starts staggering around the room clutching her throat. Janet follows her around hitting her on the back. David jumps up and tries to help. Tina, Mary and Jack run into dining room)

JACK   Whatever's up?
JANET   My mother's choking.
DAVID   I think she's got a sausage roll stuck in her throat.
JACK   *(Aside)* It must have been a big one.
TINA   *(Rushing around in a panic)* My last boyfriend was a first-aider and he said the golden rule is not to panic.
JACK   *(Calming Tina down)* Okay, we're all calm, so what do we do now?
TINA   I've no idea. You see he spent all his time practising the kiss of life on me. Perhaps you should try that on Mrs Braithwaite.
JACK   *(Looking horrified)* Don't look at me. *(Pause)* I mean, you need to be qualified to do that short of thing.

(Marjorie continues to stagger about trying to get her breath)

MARY   We'd better phone for an ambulance.
JACK   That's no good, by the time they've arrived she'll have croaked it.
DAVID   This is serious. *(Aside)* She hasn't made out her will yet.
TINA   She's going all blue. I remember now, my boyfriend said that was the second golden rule. *(Rushing around in a panic)* "Once they've gone blue, they're going to black out."
MARY   Tina, would you please shut up about your boyfriend's golden rules.
JANET   Oh Mother, please stay with us. *(Pause)* Surely someone knows what to do.

(Marjorie continues to stagger about trying to get her breath)

JACK   Why don't we hang her upside down? It's what they do with babies when something's stuck.

JANET   Don't you even think of hanging my mother upside down.

(Sara and Duncan enter from hall wearing sixties clothes)

SARA   What's happening?

JANET   My mother's choking.

DUNCAN   Don't panic.

TINA   That's just what I said. *(To Janet)* He must have studied the golden rules.

DUNCAN   I'll soon clear your airway, Mrs Braithwaite.

(Duncan gets behind Marjorie. He puts his arms around her stomach, grips his hands together and gives Marjorie's stomach a hard squeeze. The sausage roll flies out of Marjorie's mouth)

MARJORIE   Ah... I'm going to sue this place for every penny they've got.

DAVID   *(Sarcastically)* She's obviously made a full recovery.

JACK   We've all been very worried about you, Mrs Braithwaite.

MARJORIE   *(To Jack)* Not half as worried as you'll be when I've seen my solicitor.

JANET   *(Kissing Duncan)* Thank you so much. You've saved my mother's life.

SARA   Duncan's a first-aider. He's always repairing broken bones on the rugby field.

MARJORIE   *(Sitting down – gasping for breath)* Don't all stand there, get me a glass of water.

DAVID   *(Aside)* She's back to her normal self.

(Tina runs into the kitchen and pours out a glass of water. Mary starts fanning Marjorie with a newspaper)

MARJORIE   *(Looking at Jack)* You've not heard the last of this.

JACK   You can't blame me, madam. Those sausage rolls were freshly baked today.

MARJORIE   What ingredients did you use, concrete?

DAVID   I don't think it's anyone's fault.

MARJORIE   I knew I wouldn't get any backing from you.

(Tina goes into dining room with a glass of water. Marjorie snatches it, and gulps it down. Jack picks up sausage roll with a tissue)

JACK   *(Examining sausage roll)* Just as I thought, cooked to perfection. *(Throws sausage roll in bin. It makes a loud bang)*

JANET   You look much better now, Mum.

MARJORIE   I'm going to my room.

JANET   Right, I'll take you.

MARJORIE   No, you stay with your husband. *(Sarcastically to Janet)* I don't want you spoiling your evening because of me. *(To Sara)* Perhaps you'd help me, dear.

SARA   Well, yes of course we will.

DUNCAN   I'll get this side. *(Duncan and Sara arm Marjorie out through hall exit)*

JACK   All's well that ends well. *(Pause)* Let the festivities continue. *(Tina, Mary and Jack go into kitchen)*

JANET   This is all your fault.

DAVID   You can't blame me. It was just an unfortunate accident.

JANET   Accident? You launched into my mother with a verbal attack. That was no accident.

DAVID   Look, she choked on a sausage roll, and now she's fine.

JANET   My mother was lucky she didn't die.

DAVID   *(Aside)* They say the devil looks after his own.

JANET   You seem to delight in my mother's misfortune.

DAVID   What do you mean?

JANET   You stood by and watched her being savaged by a rodent. You did nothing when she was asphyxiated. You didn't even...

DAVID   Let's get things into perspective. It'd take more than a mouse or a sausage roll to finish your mum off.

JANET   That's right, poke fun. *(Pause)* This holiday's been a catalogue of disasters for Mother.

DAVID   Well she didn't have to come.

JANET   *(Shouting)* You would have liked that wouldn't you?

DAVID   *(Shouting)* She's done it again. Your mum's driving a wedge between us. She's split our marriage down the middle. *(Pause)* Can't you remember how blissfully happy we were before she moved in?

JANET   Circumstances change. We can't live in the past.

DAVID   I wouldn't mind her staying with us, if she was a normal human being.

JANET   That's not fair.

DAVID   What's wrong with looking round some old folks homes?

JANET   I couldn't do it.

DAVID   Two minutes ago we both agreed to make a fresh start.

JANET   Just don't ask me to choose between you and Mother.

DAVID   *(Getting cross)* But I'm your husband.
JANET   *(Getting cross)* Yes, and she's my mother.

(David and Janet sit in silence on opposite sides of the room. Sara and Duncan enter from hall)

   (To Sara) How's Mother?
SARA   Absolutely fine. She's having a lie down.
JANET   I'll never be able to thank you enough.
DUNCAN   It was nothing.
JANET   You're too modest by half. *(Looking at David)* Thank goodness someone knew what they were doing.

(Mary, Tina and Jack go into dining room)

JACK   We're very privileged to have in our midst tonight a couple who've returned to celebrate their second honeymoon after thirty-two years of blissfully happy marriage. I'm now going to ask the happy couple to start an excuse-me dance to their very special tune.
TINA   I've just had a brilliant idea. Let's have a competition and make the worst dancer pay a forfeit.
DUNCAN   I've never been any good at dancing.
TINA   *(Looking pleased)* Oh dear, what a pity. *(Pause)* Can I be the judge, and think of a forfeit?
JACK   That's fine by me. *(Jack puts on a CD of 'How do you do it?' by Gerry and the Pacemakers.)* If the happy couple would start us off, please, to the tune that means so much to them.

(David and Janet dance. After twenty seconds, David and Janet select new partners. David chooses Mary and Janet chooses Jack. After another twenty seconds, David chooses Sara and Janet chooses Duncan. Jack and Mary dance together. Duncan now does his own thing. He goes around the room dancing with everyone. He thinks he is John Travolta. Janet takes David to one side of dining room. Tina makes notes on a piece of paper)

JANET   I'm going to my room. I've got some serious thinking to do.
DAVID   Let's go and sort things out together.
JANET   After what you've been saying, I can't even see us staying together.
DAVID   Please don't go. *(Pause)* I'm sorry.

(The music fades low. Everyone stops dancing. Janet exits to hall)

47

TINA   After careful deliberation, I've picked Duncan. And as a forfeit he's got to do ten press-ups.

(David sits down and starts drinking heavily)

JACK   *(To Mary)* You'd better be the umpire to make sure there's no foul play.

(Duncan gets himself onto the floor and is about to start)

TINA   *(To Duncan)* No resting between each press-up, and make sure your arms are straight.
MARY   *(To Duncan)* Off you go.

(Duncan starts to do the press-ups, and everybody counts. Tina looks worried. By the time he has got to seven, he is having problems)

SARA   Whatever's up with you? *(Duncan goes for number eight. By now he is really struggling)* Get on with it, stop messing about, Duncan.
DUNCAN   *(Gasping for breath)* You've worn me out. I've nothing left to offer. *(Duncan completes the eighth press-up and goes for nine)*
JACK   Come on, just two more. *(Duncan completes his ninth press up)* Yes, yes. One to go. *(At this point Tyson runs under Duncan and sits down)*
TINA   Stop, Tyson's under you. You'll crush him.

(Duncan jumps up and hides behind Tina)

JACK   *(To Duncan)* What do you think you're doing?
TINA   Tyson, where are you?

(Duncan cowers behind Tina. Tyson runs through hall exit)

MARY   There he goes, back into the hall.
TINA   We'll have to start all over again.
JACK   Oh no we won't, the boy's only got one more press-up to go.
TINA   But he's been resting. That's not fair.
MARY   As the official judge, I declare the contest null and void.
TINA   I'm happy.
JACK   I'm satisfied. *(Shaking hands with Tina)*
DUNCAN   *(Shouting)* I'm knackered.
SARA   *(To Duncan)* You'd better sit down for a while, you've gone white.

(Sara and Duncan sit at table. Toni Clark enters from hall)

48

JACK   *(To Tina)* Whatever's that woman doing here?

TINA   We're going out for a drink.

JACK   *(Aside – to Tina)* I can't believe you'd fraternise with the enemy.

TONI   Hello, Mr Longthorp.

JACK   *(Abruptly)* Hello.

TONI   *(To Jack)* Don't forget I'm calling in tomorrow to make my final assessment.

JACK   *(Sarcastically)* I can hardly wait.

TONI   I hope everything's shipshape, it'd be a shame to see this place closed down.

JACK   *(Angrily)* Why don't you find yourself a proper job? Then we could all get …

TINA   *(To Toni)* Would you like a drink?

TONI   I'd love an orange, please. *(Tina pours Toni a drink)*

MARY   *(To Jack)* I'm going to sort out the linen for tomorrow. *(Exits to hall)*

TINA   *(Handing Toni her drink)* It's on the house.

(Jack puts on a CD of Cliff Richard singing 'The Next Time')

JACK   *(To Tina)* You what?

TONI   Cheers.

TINA   They made some great records in the sixties.

TONI   This is one of my mum's all time favourites. *(Looking at Tina with interest)* Fancy a dance?

TINA   Yea, why not? *(Toni and Tina dance, the music fades down low)*

SARA   You look much better now, Duncan.

DUNCAN   Please don't tell my mates I couldn't do ten press-ups.

SARA   You could have done them easily if Tyson hadn't got in the way.

DUNCAN   Actually, I think he may have saved my reputation. *(Pause)* I'm ready for bed.

SARA   I suppose we have got a long journey tomorrow.

DUNCAN   I wasn't thinking of going to sleep.

SARA   Brilliant. Come on let's go for it.

(Sara and Duncan run through hall exit. Jack sits by David who is drinking heavily)

DAVID   Can I buy you a drink?

JACK   No thanks. I've got an early start tomorrow. *(Pause)* Has your second honeymoon lived up to expectations?

49

DAVID   I was hoping we'd rekindle forgotten feelings. But we've drifted apart. Arguing's the only thing we're any good at now.

JACK   That's no different than most married couples.

DAVID   *(Slurring his words)* My wife's changed. She's not the girl I married.

JACK   You know what they say about marriage. For the first six months you could eat your wife, and for the rest of your life you wish you had.

DAVID   We're never alone to sort things out now the mother-in-law's living with us.

JACK   You could always find a suitable old folk's home, and pop her into a taxi.

DAVID   I'd rather pop her into a taxidermist.

(Toni and Tina stop dancing)

TINA   *(To Jack)* Toni's taking me to the *Starlight Club*.

TONI   I'll see you in the morning, Mr Longthorp. Let's hope I'm going to be pleasantly surprised.

JACK   *(Aside)* Let's hope one day you'll be unpleasantly surprised by an approaching express train.

TINA   Keep an eye open for Tyson, bye. *(Exits to hall with Toni)*

DAVID   How I yearn to be young again, with all that zest for life. *(Pause)* You never realise what age does to you, till you get old.

JACK   It's no good living in the past, it's the future that's important.

DAVID   *(Sadly)* What future?

JACK   I've got to get things ready for our new guests tomorrow. *(Pause)* Will you be okay?

DAVID   I'll be fine.

(Jack switches off some of the lights, leaving the room dimly lit)

JACK   Help yourself to drinks, on the house.

DAVID   Thanks.

(Jack exits to hall. David looks through CDs and puts on The Beatles singing either 'All You Need is Love' or, 'If I Fell'. He sits down and continues drinking heavily. Amina enters from hall. She is wearing sixties clothes)

AMINA   Hi!

DAVID   Hello, you're a bit late, the party's over.

AMINA   I had an article I wanted to get off. That's the trouble with being a workaholic.

DAVID   Would you like a drink? I'm ready for a double.

AMINA   I'd love a scotch please. *(Pause)* Where's your wife?

DAVID   *(Pouring out two drinks)* She's gone to bed. *(Handing Amina her drink)*

AMINA   Thank you. *(Pause)* To the good times.

DAVID   Cheers.

(Amina and David take a long drink)

AMINA   So what are your plans now?

DAVID   I've no idea.

AMINA   Do they include me?

DAVID   Yesterday was a moment of madness. I should have known better.

AMINA   It was a moment in heaven for me.

DAVID   I'm very flattered. But it was just a kiss.

AMINA   *(Looking sad)* So it meant nothing to you?

DAVID   Are you joking? My whole life flashed before my eyes. By the time we'd finished, I was a recycled teenager.

AMINA   That's one of the nicest compliments anyone's ever paid me. *(Looking vague)* I think.

DAVID   *(Slurring his words)* That's the problem with being married for thirty-two years. The passion dulls and the desire fades. *(Pause for drink)* It's only when you experience the sensual thrill of kissing French chips, I mean fresh lips, that long forgotten feelings are aroused. *(Amina holds David's hands)*

AMINA   Everyone needs a bit of romance in their lives.

DAVID   I shouldn't be saying all this. *(Having another long drink)* It must be the drink talking.

AMINA   My paper's transferring me to our New York office, and they're doubling my salary.

DAVID   Congratulations.

AMINA   I'm not looking for praise, I'm looking for a partner.

DAVID   *(Looking surprised)* You mean, you're inviting me along?

AMINA   There's never been any other man who I've wanted to share my life with.

DAVID   You're basing all this on a teenager's crush.

AMINA   *(Smiling seductively)* From the moment we met again, I realised nothing had changed. All those magical feelings came flooding back.

DAVID   You make it all sound so simple.

AMINA   That's because I've already made up my mind. *(Pause)* It was fate that drew us together. We can't let this opportunity slip away.

DAVID   I've never cheated on my wife. *(Pause)* I'm a member of the church choir. *(Pause)* What will the vicar say?

AMINA   *(Getting close to David)* I love you, let's go to bed.

DAVID   Somehow, I don't think he'll be saying that.

AMINA   What's the point of life if you can't get pleasure from it? *(Kisses David passionately)* It's the last evening of your holiday. Time to throw caution to the wind. *(Pause)* Haven't you ever wanted to fulfil all your wildest fantasies?

DAVID   Middle-aged married men only do that in their dreams.

AMINA   *(Seductively)* Don't you believe it. *(Holding out her hand)* Come on.

DAVID   Just hang on a minute. I need to give this some serious thought.

AMINA   *(Walking to hall exit)* Don't take too long. *(Exits to hall)*

DAVID   *(Running through hall exit)* Wait for me.

Scene II

As the curtain rises, the stage is empty and the phone is ringing. Jack enters from hall and answers it.

JACK   Sea View guest house... *(Looking in appointment book)* I'm afraid we're fully booked in September... so it's the first week in October then, Mrs Turner... that's lovely, bye.

(Replaces receiver and writes in appointment book. He exits to hall. Janet enters from hall looking very thoughtful. She paces up and down. She starts talking to herself)

JANET   Mum, you'd better sit down. David and I are trying to save our marriage and we need some space. Did you know there's some lovely homes for the elderly? Now don't get upset. *(Pause)* You have taken your blood pressure pills, and your angina tablet, haven't you?

(Janet sits down and stares into space. The phone rings. Jack enters from hall and answers it)

JACK   Sea View guest house... Oh right... So that's two adults, and your teenage daughter... only too pleased... wonderful... I'll book you in, Mr Matthews, bye. *(Replaces receiver and writes in appointment book. He does not notice Janet. He exits to hall)*

JANET   I'm so sorry, Mum, but we've packed your suitcase, and told the milkman to cancel that extra pint.

MARY   *(Entering from hall)* Hello, have you enjoyed your second honeymoon?

JANET   *(Unconvincingly)* We've had a lovely time. *(Pause)* You haven't seen my husband I suppose?

MARY   No, perhaps he's gone for walk. *(Pause)* Fancy a cup of tea?

JANET   Any chance of a double scotch? *(Pause)* Actually a tea'll be fine thanks.

(Mary goes into kitchen and makes a tea. Marjorie enters from hall)

    Hello, Mum. Did you sleep well?

MARJORIE   Are you joking? I haven't slept all week.

MARY   *(Poking her head through kitchen door)* I'm sorry, I can't remember if you take sugar in tea?

MARJORIE   No I don't, and make sure it's got some colour this time.

JANET   No sugar for me, thanks.

MARY   Won't be a sec. *(Goes back into kitchen and pours out two teas)*

JANET   Mum, we need to have a talk. For the past ten years, while you've been living with us...

(Sara and Duncan enter from hall. They are both wearing shorts and t-shirts)

SARA   *(To Janet)* Excuse us, we've been for a swim.

JANET   You didn't see my husband I suppose?

DUNCAN   No, we had the sea to ourselves.

SARA   It's an absolutely glorious day, the sea's as warm as toast.

MARJORIE   That means it's going to be like a sauna in that car.

SARA   It's been lovely meeting you all. *(To Janet)* What's it like being married for thirty-two years?

JANET   Like most couples, we've had our problems. But if you truly love each other, things have a way of working out.

MARJORIE   *(Aside)* If you believe that, you'll believe anything.

SARA   Let's hope we'll be as happy as you are.

JACK   *(Entering from hall)* Morning all, lovely day. *(Jack picks up appointment book and goes into kitchen – to Mary)* You'll be pleased to know we've had ten bookings this morning.

MARY   We've not had ten bookings since those swingers held their Christmas Ball here.

JACK   *(Opens appointment book)* August, September, October fully booked, one week free in November. *(Pause)* The phone's been going non-stop.

MARY   I told you everything'd work out. *(Pause)* Be a dear and take these teas to Mrs Braithwaite and her daughter.

JACK   And the icing on the cake is I won't have to put up with that old bag Braithwaite any more. *(Takes the two teas and appointment book into dining room)* You're looking rather radiant this morning, Mrs Braithwaite. *(Unconvincingly)* I'd like to say it's been a privilege sharing our home with you. *(Aside)* I'd like to say that.

(Jack puts teas on table and appointment book on reception table. He then goes into kitchen)

MARJORIE   Look at the state of that tea. I can see the bottom of the cup.

SARA   We'd better get dressed.

DUNCAN   Yea, we should get on the road before the traffic gets too bad.

(Sara and Duncan exit to hall. Marjorie looks for her travel-sick pill)

JANET   Now Mum, David and I have been talking, and, well, you see, we, I mean David thinks it's probably best if…

MARJORIE   I can't find my travel-sick pill. I must have left it in the bedroom.

JANET   *(Getting frustrated)* Would you please just …

MARJORIE   You're supposed to take it at least one hour before the journey. I'm already feeling queasy. *(Exits to hall)*

TINA   *(Entering from hall carrying a newspaper)* Lovely morning.

JANET   *(Unconvincingly)* Yes, absolutely wonderful.

(Tina goes into kitchen. Janet drinks her tea)

TINA   Hi, I've got some fantastic news. *(Hands Mary the paper)*

JACK   Has that health inspector been struck down with severe food poisoning?

TINA   No, look at the top of page twenty.

MARY   *(Looking at paper, reads aloud)* "The British guest house is alive and well. Having just spent a week in a wonderful, friendly home called *Sea View*, I can thoroughly recommend a holiday in England."

TINA   The article goes on to give all our details. We couldn't have written a better advert ourselves.

JACK   *(Grabbing paper)* Whoever wrote all this?

TINA   Amina Betnay. Look, her picture's at the bottom of it. *(Pointing into the paper)*

JACK   Why did she do it? I haven't paid her a penny.

TINA   She's a top journalist, who goes around trying out holidays, and reporting on them.

JACK   *(Getting excited)* That explains why we've had all those bookings. *(Pause)* I'll go and knock five per cent off her bill.

TINA   Don't overdo it.

(Jack exits to hall with the newspaper. Marjorie enters from hall. Tina and Mary continue in silent conversation)

MARJORIE   It's a wonder I don't rattle considering the number of pills I'm forced to take. *(Taking the pill with her tea)*
    By the way I've got a bit of news.

JANET   *(Getting frustrated)* Well it'll have to wait, because what I've got to tell you won't. *(Pause)* Mum, there's no easy way to say this but...

MARJORIE   I'm moving to Tenerife.

JANET   *(With disbelief)* You what?

MARJORIE   Your father and I are getting back together.

JANET   I can't believe I'm hearing this. *(Pause)* What about the lollipop lady, are you sharing wardrobes?

MARJORIE   No, she left two years ago to join a circus.

JANET   So, how did you find out about all this?

MARJORIE   Your dad phoned last week and said he was missing me. We had a long chat, and decided to give it another go. So I'm moving to Tenerife next month. I mean, let's face facts, England's over-populated, over-priced and the weather's always overcast.

JANET   And you didn't think to tell me anything about this?

MARJORIE   I didn't want to spoil your holiday. *(Pause)* Look, I appreciate what you've done. But, for once in my life, I've got to consider myself.

JANET   I hope you're making the right decision.

MARJORIE   Of course I am. Your dad's come into a lot of money. He'll need someone to help him spend it. *(Pause)* So what was this serious talk you wanted to have?

JANET   *(Unconvincingly)* Oh well, um. I need your opinion on a new dress I've bought.

JACK   *(Entering from hall carrying a newspaper – to Janet)*
Have you heard the news? *(Looking pleased)* We've been featured
in the national press as one of the top guest houses in England.
JANET   Congratulations.
MARJORIE   That just confirms what I thought. *(Pause)* You
can't believe a word you read in the papers.
JANET   Could I have a look, please?
JACK   *(Handing paper to Janet)* Top of page twenty.

(Jack goes into kitchen. Janet reads newspaper)

Tina, would you get me another dozen copies of that paper?
TINA   What are you intending to do, wallpaper the dining room
with them?
JACK   *(Handing Tina some money)* Don't get facetious. Very
few guest houses have made the headlines in a national newspaper.

(Tina exits to hall. Jack and Mary continue in silent conversation)

JANET   It's an excellent article. Would you like to read it?
MARJORIE   No thanks. *(Pause)* I'm going to buy some
sunglasses. I'll be needing them in Tenerife.
JANET   Are you sure about all this, Mum?
MARJORIE   I intend to enjoy my last few years basking in the
sun and sipping tequilas.
JANET   David'll certainly be surprised when I tell him.
MARJORIE   He'll probably think Christmas has arrived early.
JANET   Things couldn't have worked out better. *(Looking
guilty)* I mean, for you. *(Pause)* I'll come to the shop and help you
choose your sunglasses. *(Exits to hall with Marjorie)*
JACK   We're going to hit the big times. I can see it now.
MARY   Don't get carried away, Jack.
JACK   Carried away? This guest house'll soon be the talk of the
town.
MARY   Could you give me a hand with the rooms, please?
JACK   Today, my dearest, I'll do anything you want.

*(Mary and Jack exit to hall. After a few seconds David and Amina
enter from hall. David is carrying Amina's two cases. He puts them
on the floor in the dining room)*

DAVID   Let's go into the kitchen, it'll be more private. *(Goes
into kitchen with Amina)*
AMINA   *(Hugging David)* Thank you for last night.
DAVID   *(Smiling)* The pleasure was all mine.

AMINA   Are you sure about leaving your wife? I don't want to force you into a situation you'll live to regret.

DAVID   My mother-in-law's ruined our marriage, and my wife's not prepared to do anything about it.

AMINA   *(Looking into David's eyes)* And you're happy to come to New York and live with me?

DAVID   Yes, once I've sorted things out, I'll phone you.

AMINA   So you don't want me around when you tell your wife?

DAVID   No, it's best if I speak to her alone. *(Pause)* She won't even miss me. She's too wrapped up with her mother. *(Pause)* I might as well get things moving.

AMINA   In that case, I'll leave you to it. *(Pause)* I'll be waiting for your call. *(Kissing David)* This is everything I've ever dreamed of.

(Amina kisses David. Jack enters from hall, he walks towards the kitchen. The phone rings, Jack answers it. Amina and David continue to hug and kiss)

JACK   Sea View guest house... *(Looking through appointment book)* No, I'm very sorry we're fully booked... Oh right... I can offer you next February... That's good... I'll book you in, Mrs Bowden, bye. *(Replaces receiver and writes in appointment book)*

AMINA   I'll distract him. *(Goes into dining room – to Jack)* Hi.

JACK   *(Turning to face Amina)* Ms. Betnay, or may I call you Amina?

AMINA   Amina's fine.

JACK   I've been looking for you everywhere. *(Hugging Amina)* What made you write such a glowing report on our humble guest house?

AMINA   I've had a wonderful nostalgic time, recapturing happy memories of my school days. In fact the whole week's been a turning point in my life.

(David exits to hall unseen by Jack)

JACK   *(Looking thoughtful)* Most of our guests say their stay here's been an unforgettable experience. *(Pause)* If there's anything I can ever do in return.

AMINA   There is one thing...

JACK   What is it, a follow up interview, probing the fascinating mind of an entrepreneur?

AMINA   *(Handing over her room key)* Actually, I was hoping you'd lift my cases into the car only they're rather heavy.

57

JACK   Oh, right. *(Puts her key on the board, and picks up cases)* It'll be my pleasure. And we'll be knocking five per cent off your next booking.

AMINA   *(Unconvincingly)* That's great.

(Amina and Jack exit to hall. After a few seconds Janet and Marjorie enter from hall. Marjorie is wearing sunglasses)

JANET   *(To Marjorie)* I'm getting very worried about David. It's unlike him to disappear without saying a word.

MARJORIE   Perhaps he's got himself another girl friend. His track record's not been very good this week.

JANET   Don't be ridiculous, Mum. They were misunderstandings.

MARJORIE   Men can't help it. Their brains are wired down to their y-fronts, and everything short circuits when a pretty girl appears.

JANET   I trust David implicitly.

MARJORIE   If only you'd chosen a husband with the feel-good-factor.

JANET   Sorry?

MARJORIE   You feel good when you see his bank balance. You feel good about his social position. You feel good about his future prospects. You feel…

JANET   And what about feeling good with him as a partner?

MARJORIE   That comes way down the list.

JANET   You've got it all wrong, Mum. *(David enters from hall)* It's love that counts. *(To David)* Where the hell have you been?

MARJORIE   *(Sarcastically)* I'll leave you two lovebirds to it. *(Exits to hall)*

DAVID   I couldn't sleep so I went for a walk along the beach.

JANET   And whatever time did you come to bed last night?

DAVID   *(Looking guilty)* I'm not sure. I'd had a few drinks.

JANET   You've hardly spoken for the last few days. Then you go off on some transcendental meditation trip. What's the matter with you?

DAVID   You'd better sit down. Something's happened that's going to affect our future.

(Tina enters from hall. She is carrying a dozen newspapers. She hands one to David)

TINA   Here, check out page twenty. There's a fantastic write up on our guest house.

DAVID   *(Totally uninterested)* Really, I'm very pleased for you.

(Tina goes into kitchen and reads paper)

   Look for the past ten years, while your mother's been living with us, we've had some good times, but...

JACK   *(Entering from hall)* What do you think about the article?

DAVID   *(Looking vague)* Article?... Oh yes... Um, it's very good.

JACK   Of course it's no more than we deserve. We've set the standards that others strive to reach. You see...

DAVID   If you don't mind, I'd like to have a word with my wife, in private.

JACK   Oh, right I'll leave you to it then. *(Exits to hall)*

DAVID   Now where was I?

JANET   Reminding me what a wonderful life we've had together. *(Lovingly)* I suppose you're going to say the next thirty years'll be even better.

(Amina enters from hall carrying her handbag.)

DAVID   *(Aside – to Amina)* You're a bit premature. I was just about to break the news.

AMINA   Oh dear, bad timing. *(Opening her handbag)* I've found a hitch-hiker in my handbag. *(Getting Tyson out of her handbag and giving him a stroke)* I'd stopped at the traffic lights and heard this squealing. The next thing was, Tyson popped his head out. *(Amina takes Tyson into the kitchen)* I've brought Tyson back. He'd got into my handbag.

TINA   *(Shouting)* Tyson, you've come home to Mummy. Oh, you dear thing. *(To Amina)* Thank you so much.

(Amina and Tina continue in silent conversation. They make a fuss of Tyson)

JANET   *(To David)* You'd better check our room's empty before we leave.

DAVID   *(Getting frustrated)* Forget the room, we need to have a talk.

JANET   We'll have plenty of time in the car. Now be a dear and have a check round.

DAVID   Oh, all right. *(Exits to hall)*

TINA   *(Taking Tyson from Amina – to Tyson)* Did he go for a ride in a big motor car then? *(Moving into the dining room)* Come along with Tina and she'll put you back in your little cage and hide you in the cupboard under the stairs where the nasty health inspector won't find you. *(Exits to hall)*

(Amina goes into dining room)

JANET   Hello, we haven't been introduced. I'm Janet.

AMINA   Amina Betney.

JANET   Amina, what a lovely name. *(Pause)* I see from your article you've had a good week.

AMINA   Yes, it's been great thanks. *(Walking to hall exit)* I really must be going.

JANET   It must be very rewarding, having thousands of people hang on your every word in the press.

AMINA   *(Turning to face Janet)* Well, it has its moments.

JANET   I've never been a career woman. I had three children, they kept me busy.

AMINA   I'm sure they did.

JANET   They've all left home. Now it's just mother who's living with us.

AMINA   Really.

JANET   Ageing parents can cause more trouble than kids. *(Pause)* My mother's caused all sorts of problems in my marriage, but that's all sorted now. She's moving to Tenerife to live with Dad.

AMINA   Oh, right.

JANET   That'll give David and me a chance to get to know each other again. *(Pause)* We came here to celebrate our second honeymoon. I've been married to the most wonderful man for thirty-two years.

AMINA   You obviously love him a lot.

JANET   I daren't imagine life without him.

AMINA   *(Aside)* Oh dear.

JANET   He's my best friend, my strength, my support. In fact he's my whole world. Do you know I could forgive him for anything.

AMINA   Well, actually ... Um ... never mind.

JANET   Is everything all right?

AMINA   Yes, fine thanks. *(Thoughtfully)* It's been nice meeting you.

JANET   And you. Hope all goes well with the job.

SARA   *(Entering from hall with Duncan)* I wish we were staying here for another week.

DUNCAN   I've got to get back to work. *(Aside)* I need the rest.

TINA   *(Entering from hall with Jack)* I want a photo of everyone with Tyson.

JACK   Is this really necessary?

TINA   Too true, Tyson's played a major role in this week's events. Come on I'll get my camera and we'll take it outside.

(Sara, Duncan, Tina, Jack and Janet exit to hall. Amina sits on a chair, looking thoughtful. After a few seconds David enters from hall)

DAVID   Hi.

AMINA   I can't go through with this. *(Pause)* I'm so sorry, but I'm calling it off.

DAVID   Calling it off? *(Pause)* You come into my life, entice me into your bed, and after a night of sexual gymnastics, you calmly announce we're finished.

AMINA   I've just been talking to your wife. It's uncomfortable meeting face to face and realizing the consequences of your actions. *(Pause)* What are your honest thoughts about me?

DAVID   You're attractive, vibrant, intelligent, kind. *(Pause)* What more can I say?

AMINA   That you love me?

DAVID   I've hardly had chance to get to know you.

AMINA   You're going with me for all the wrong reasons. You wanted the excitement of a fling. You're angry with your wife. *(Pause)* Look I adore you, but a one-sided love affair always ends in heartbreak.

DAVID   *(Getting cross)* This was supposed to be my second honeymoon. You've turned my whole week upside down.

AMINA   You've turned my whole world upside down.

DAVID   My marriage is over, my mother-in-law's seen to that.

AMINA   She's moving to Tenerife to live with her husband.

DAVID   Who told you that?

AMINA   Your wife. *(Pause)* You can sort things out now.

DAVID   So that's it then? *(Getting cross)* I don't even get a say in any of this?

AMINA   *(Reflectively)* If only I hadn't brought Tyson back, things could have turned out so differently.

DAVID   You can't let our future plans be decided by a rodent.

AMINA   Sometimes things just aren't meant to be.

DAVID   Look, let's just …

AMINA   I'm moving to New York next month and devoting all my energy to work. In five years I'll be the editor of our paper.

DAVID   And you'll soon forget all about me.

AMINA   *(Seductively)* I'll cherish the memory of our time together for the rest of my life.

JANET   *(Entering from hall)* You both missed the photo-session.

DAVID   *(Getting cross)* What photo-session?

AMINA   I've got to go.

DAVID   *(Aside – to Amina)* You can't just walk out like that.

(Amina exits to hall. David slumps into a chair and stares into space)

JANET   Are you all right, David?

SARA   *(Entering from hall with Duncan)* We're just off.

DUNCAN   I've got a rugby game this afternoon.

SARA   I don't want you overdoing it, Duncan.

DUNCAN   After what I've been through this week, believe me, it'll be a doddle.

JANET   Have a safe journey home.

SARA   Thank you for all your advice, David. Best of luck for the future.

JANET   You both look after yourselves.

SARA   We'll come back here one day for our second honeymoon.

DUNCAN   You'd better give me plenty of warning.

(Marjorie enters from hall)

SARA   Good-bye, Mrs Braithwaite.

MARJORIE   You can call me Marjorie. Nice to have met you both.

(Sara and Duncan put their room key on the board and then exit to hall)

JANET   Are you ready to go, Mum?

MARJORIE   I'll just pop a note in the visitors' book. *(Writing in visitors' book)* How do you spell inedible?

JANET   Mother, don't you dare.

MARJORIE   I'll say that the food was different. *(Putting her key on the board)* I'll wait in the car. *(Exits to hall)*

JANET   You never did tell me what you had to say that was so urgent.

DAVID   *(Very quietly)* We've come very close to splitting up this week.

JANET   This second honeymoon's made me realise just how precious you are to me.

DAVID   And you don't think it's too late to save our marriage?

JANET   We've been through too much together to throw it all away.

DAVID   *(Quietly)* I'm willing to give it another go if you are.

JANET   *(Looking around the room)* Thirty-two years ago we were in this very room with our whole lives in front of us.

DAVID   Blissfully unaware of what life was going to throw at us.

JANET   I think you'll find the future's going to be much brighter from now on. *(Kissing David)*

DAVID   We never did get to renew our marriage vows.

JANET   Let's do it now.

(Janet and David go into kitchen and write in the cupboard. The phone rings. Tina enters from the hall and answers the phone)

TINA   Hello... What?... You're kidding... You're not... You are... Yes, certainly. Bye. *(Replaces receiver and runs to the hall exit)* Jack, Mary, come here quickly.

(Meanwhile David points to something in the bottom of the cupboard. Janet looks and then shuts the cupboard door quickly. They start searching the other cupboards)

JACK   *(Entering from hall with Mary)* Whatever's wrong?

TINA   *(Getting excited)* That was Steve Wright on the phone. He spotted our article in the paper and he's decided to have a weekend break here next year.

JACK   You're having a laugh aren't you?

TINA   No, and he's going to give us a mention on his radio show.

MARY   That's wonderful. Things couldn't have worked out better.

(David and Janet go into dining room)

DAVID   Thank you for everything. *(Writing in visitors' book)*

JANET   We'll be back sometime in the future for our third honeymoon.

JACK   Book early to avoid disappointment.

JANET   There's just one thing. Tyson, the mouse, is a girl.

JACK   You what?

JANET   She's had at least ten babies. The nest's in your kitchen cupboard under the microwave.

DAVID   *(Putting their key on the board and going off into the hall arm-in-arm with Janet)* Best of luck.

JACK   I might have guessed that something like this would happen.

TINA *(Reassuringly)* Don't worry. I'll get a box and pop the nest into it. *(Exits into hall)*

(Jack and Mary go into the kitchen and start looking in the cupboard. Toni enters from the hall carrying a briefcase. She rings the service bell. Jack and Mary close the cupboard door quickly and return to the dining room)

TONI   Good morning. I'm here to make my final inspection.

MARY   I'll leave you to it, dear. *(Exits to hall)*

JACK   If you take a seat, I'll make you a nice cup of coffee.

TONI   I haven't got time now, thank you.

JACK   Actually there's been a slight hiccup.

TONI   You've had ample time to sort out any hiccups. I made it perfectly clear that today was the deadline.

JACK   *(Putting his arm on Toni's shoulder)* Look, can't we talk about this?

TONI   *(Removing Jack's arm)* If you want this guest house to remain open, I'd better be impressed with what I find. *(Goes into kitchen and starts to make notes. Tina enters from the hall with a box)*

JACK   You're too late. The Gestapo's arrived. Once she finds that mouse nest, we'll be closed down.

TINA   We can't give up that easily. *(Puts box on a table)*

JACK   If I was twenty years younger, had all my own teeth, hair and good looks, I might be able to reason with her.

TINA   That wouldn't make any difference.

JACK   You're probably right. That woman hasn't got any feelings.

TINA   *(Aside)* That's where you're wrong. *(To Jack)* Leave this to me.

(Tina goes into the kitchen and goes directly to the cupboard and stands with her back to it. There follows a mimed conversation with Toni during which Tina makes desperate efforts to divert Toni's attention from the cupboard. Meanwhile the phone rings. Jack answers it)

JACK   Sea View guest house ... Speaking ... Oh, the Grand Hotel ... Thanks for the tip-off the other day ... I'm afraid it doesn't look too good. I'm expecting her to close us down ... Yeah, they should be shot at birth ... Right, thanks for your good wishes ... I'll let you know, bye. *(Replaces receiver)*

(In the meantime, Toni gets a certificate from her briefcase and writes on it. She goes into the dining room)

TONI   *(Handing certificate to Jack)* Here you are Mr Longthorp.

JACK   What's this, a closing down notification?

TONI   No, it's a certificate of excellence. *(Pause)* I'm very impressed. Keep up the good work.

JACK   *(In a state of shock)* Thank you.

TONI   I'll see myself out. Good day.

(Toni exits to hall. In the meantime, Tina fetches a bottle of champagne from the fridge, pours three glasses, places them on a tray and leaves it on a cabinet by the door)

JACK   *(To Tina as she enters the dining room)* What are you, some sort of miracle worker? *(Pause)* If you'd been a bloke I might have understood it.

TINA   It's fortunate I'm not a bloke. *(In a whisper)* Strictly between ourselves, she fancies me. She's putty in my hands.

JACK   You mean she's …?

TINA   Sure is. Mind you, all the same, it wasn't easy. I had a dreadful time in there, keeping her away from that mouse nest.

MARY   *(Entering from hall)* So when are we being closed down?

JACK   We're not. *(Holding up certificate)* We've even got a certificate of excellence. This is turning out to be the best day of my life. We're going to be rich and famous.

TINA   *(Looking in the visitors' book)* Listen to what David Thompson's written – "Please thank Tyson for saving my marriage."

MARY   Whatever does he mean?

TINA   I've no idea, but I think Tyson's brought us all some good luck this week.

JACK   You could be right.

TINA   This calls for a celebration. *(She goes into the kitchen and returns, at once, with the tray which she puts on the sideboard and hands the glasses to Mary and Jack)* Right – first of all, let's drink a toast to Amina whose article has brought us lots of bookings.

ALL   To Amina! *(They all raise their glasses and drink)*

JACK   *(Winking at Tina)* And I'd like to drink a toast to our friendly health inspector, who's become very accommodating. *(Aside – to Tina)* Thanks to you, Tina.

ALL   To Toni! *(They all raise their glasses and drink)*

MARY   And we mustn't forget Tyson. After all, she did save the Thompson's marriage.

TINA   She's my hero. Wait – I'll go and fetch her. *(Exits to hall)*

JACK   Well, Mary, it looks as if we've finally cracked it. From now on it's going to be plain sailing.

MARY I think you could be right, darling. Especially if we're going to get a bit of publicity on the radio.

JACK *(Giving Mary a hug)* It was a near thing though, wasn't it. If that health inspector had looked in the cupboard and found those mice, we would…

TINA *(Entering from the hall waving an empty mouse cage)* I don't believe it. Tyson's not in her cage.

(Mary, Tina and Jack start looking around the dining room)

JACK Please tell me this isn't happening.

MARY Don't panic, there she is, running into the hall.

(Tyson's boyfriend runs through hall exit. Mary points to the hall exit)

JACK That's not Tyson, it's the wrong colour.

TINA Oh, how sweet. Tyson's found herself a little boyfriend. This could be the start of another holiday romance.

MARY And you know what that means.

JACK *(Shouting)* They'll be producing thousands more little Tysons. They'll be everywhere. *(Pause)* I can see the headlines in the paper now, "Guest house renamed *Rodents' Retreat*".

MARY Calm down, Jack. *(Grabbing a frying pan from the kitchen)*

JACK *(Shouting)* Calm down. I'll kill that bloody mouse if it's the last thing I do.

(Jack runs through hall exit carrying the frying pan above his head)

MARY Come back here, Jack.

TINA Don't do it, Mr Longthorp.

(Mary and Tina exit to hall. Tyson and her boyfriend run across the dining room together)

BLACKOUT